THE LITURGICAL MOVEMENT

IS VOLUME

115

OF THE

Twentieth Century Encyclopedia of Catholicism

UNDER SECTION

X

THE WORSHIP OF THE CHURCH

IT IS ALSO THE

118TH

VOLUME IN ORDER OF PUBLICATION

Edited by HENRI DANIEL-ROPS *of the Académie Française*

THE LITURGICAL MOVEMENT

By *The Sacerdotal Communities
of Saint-Severin of Paris
and Saint-Joseph of Nice*

Translated from the French by LANCELOT SHEPPARD

HAWTHORN BOOKS · PUBLISHERS · *New York*

First Edition, April, 1964

NIHIL OBSTAT

Joannes M. T. Barton, S.T.D., L.S.S.

   Censor Deputatus

IMPRIMATUR

✠ Georgius L. Craven

   Episcopus Sebastopolis, Vicarius Generalis

Westmonasterii, die XVII MARTII MCMLXIV

The Nihil obstat and Imprimatur are a declaration that a book or pamphlet is
considered to be free from doctrinal or moral error. It is not implied that those
who have granted the Nihil obstat and Imprimatur agree with the contents,
opinions, or statements expressed.

H-9560

CONTENTS

PART II: FUNDAMENTAL IDEAS OF THE LITURGICAL REVIVAL

PART III: THE PRINCIPAL ADVANCES MADE BY THE LITURGICAL RENEWAL

PART I

SHORT HISTORY OF THE
LITURGICAL MOVEMENT

The liturgical movement came into being because it was necessary. Under the influence of modern individualism and rationalism, the worship of the Church with its magnificent forms, lofty considerations and concentration on the totality of revealed realities, had been increasingly relegated to the background. Spiritual life had assumed very largely a subjective and private character. It therefore became necessary that from within the Church should arise the desire to regain what had been thus set aside. Scientific and historical research was then carried out in an endeavour to revive the liturgy in its purity and to restore to it the place belonging to it in religious life. But there soon arose a further tendency to attribute to it an importance that it does not possess. . . .

(Letter from Romano Guardini to the bishop
of Mainz, 1940)[1]

A remark that holds good for the whole of this short book requires to be emphasized in regard to this first part. In a concern for clarity the subject has been divided up into sections—their artificial nature will strike the reader at once— dealing with monastic influences, research institutes and parochial and youth movements. This distinction, which is based on the very rough historical succession of events in the liturgical renewal, should not cause us to forget the interpenetration that has fortunately taken place between the various elements in this renewal. And it must not be lost sight of that

[1] *La Maison-Dieu* 3, pp. 7–24. (*La Maison-Dieu* is hereafter quoted as *MD*, followed by volume and page numbers.)

the movement which began in the monasteries, together with the institutes and centres specializing in pastoral liturgy, still continues to make its contribution to the generality of parochial and other communities in a kind of continual "circumincession". It is only for reasons of method that the three following chapters have here been separated, and this separation, as will be seen, is very relative.

CHAPTER I

MONASTIC SCHOOLS

At the very beginning of his Encyclical *Mediator Dei et hominum*[1] Pius XII pointed out the essential part played by monks in the liturgical renewal. This official acknowledgement has led us to begin this history of the liturgical movement with its monastic origins and, at the end of this chapter, in order to present an unbiased account, to point out its limitations as well as its beneficial results. In company with Fr Bouyer, Dom Olivier Rousseau and a large number of recent monographs about the liturgical movement, we go back to Dom Guéranger, although the history of the liturgical movement in the proper sense of the term might be seen to begin with Pius X and Dom Lambert Beauduin.

DOM GUÉRANGER AND SOLESMES

At Solesmes is to be found what at the birth of the liturgical movement can be called its original sin. But it must at once be added that it was a *felix culpa*. At Solesmes, in fact, began the general movement which has led to a renewal of divine worship, even though at present this movement is contriving to correct and, in some sense, to deny its origins.

After ordination to the priesthood for the secular clergy Dom Guéranger (1805–75) restored the abbey of Solesmes in the Sarthe *département* in France and sought to re-establish in this peaceful corner of the country an outpost of Roman Catholicism by a fervent return to the Middle Ages as to the golden age and the ideal period of Christendom. Thus his

[1] Hereafter quoted as *Mediator*.

action was influenced by the philosophical traditionalism of the period and neo-Gothic romanticism. It was also inspired by fierce opposition to the neo-Gallicanism of the times and, generally speaking, by systematic disparagement of everything that was not strictly "Roman". These extreme positions profoundly influenced the liturgical outlook of the first abbot of Solesmes and were blemishes on the two great works that he bequeathed us—his *Institutions liturgiques* and especially his *Année liturgique* (recently republished). Dom Guéranger's work belonged to the category of what has come to be termed "archeologism", since this tendency was stigmatized expressly by the Encyclical *Mediator*. It lays itself open to the reproach, also, that the apparently spiritual and theological tendency of this reform can be seen to be at the same time the expression of a certain policy dubbed reactionary by its opponents and still supported by a certain section of the Catholics in France and elsewhere.

Apart from these controversial aspects of the movement which originated at Solesmes its more authentic and positive implications should be acknowledged. In the eyes of the historian of the Church Dom Guéranger must be given the great credit for having caused the liturgy to be known again and loved; for having restored it to a worthy, sober and really religious style; for having put forward the Roman liturgy as a model, for him the only model, and an especially privileged one and worthy of imitation; for having laid the foundations for the restoration of liturgical chant and its re-introduction into worship; finally, by his return to certain forms of worship in the Roman Church which, though in a special category, bear the stamp of universality, for being the promoter, despite himself, it is true, of ecumenism. Indeed, it requires to be said that he had no idea at all of the legitimate liturgical and disciplinary diversity in the Church; the Eastern Churches, even those in union with Rome, he regarded in their rites and customs as merely tolerated by the Roman Church.[2]

[2] Cf. H. Chirat's review of Dom Rousseau's *Histoire du mouvement liturgique* (Paris, 1945; English translation, *Progress of the Liturgy*,

BEURON AND THE WOLTER BROTHERS

The liturgical movement which grew up in Germany with the new Benedictine Congregation of Beuron was in the beginning modelled on that of Solesmes. Nevertheless, it received additional and probably more authentic inspiration from the work of Möhler (1796–1838), the theologian, who was the promoter of the patristic revival at the theological faculty of the university of Tübingen. This revival Möhler successfully combined with a strong love of the Church and with tradition as a whole; as a result, without himself being directly interested in the liturgy, he endowed the movement, which drew inspiration from him in this matter, with a more solid foundation than that formed by Solesmes's attachment to medieval forms.

All the same it is true that the two Wolter brothers, priests of Cologne who became Benedictines as Dom Maur and Dom Placid respectively, achieved a satisfactory combination of the heritage received from Dom Guéranger, in whose abbey they made their novitiate, with—in reaction to the *Aufklärung*—a

---

Westminster, Md, 1951) in *MD* 7, 137–47: "Dom Guéranger states that the Holy See has taken the oriental rites under its protection (he refers to acts of Pius IX and Gregory XVI). . . . These measures appear to him to be inspired principally by pure condescendence and by reasons of expediency. They are aimed at not embittering or wounding the peoples who practise these liturgies and it is 'to make this invitation more pressing', to 'avoid every pretext which could postpone the longed for day of reunion' that 'Rome . . . does not cease to evince her motherly regard for these liturgies . . . enshrined in languages very different from her own'. The apostolic see, he does not hesitate to write, 'has been excessively tactful . . . in the face of the susceptibilities of these unfortunate peoples, by taking under her protection the Eastern liturgies'. The Eastern liturgies appear to him as 'barriers' which make 'more difficult' the duty of 'remaining united to the centre of Catholic communion' although 'this fidelity is always possible with the help of divine grace'. In spite of their venerable antiquity they are 'make-shift', compromises, even 'a misfortune for those Churches which do not share in the Roman liturgy'. He feels himself authorized to 'think that a time will come when the language of Rome, like her faith, will be for the East, as for the West, the only means of unity and regeneration'." (References in the review quoted above.)

concern for the revival of patristic tradition. The elder brother compiled what amounts to an anthology of the Fathers in his *Praecipua ordinis monastici elementa*; there should also be mentioned his commentary on the psalms in five volumes (*Psallite sapienter*); this, too, is full of quotations from the Fathers.

MAREDSOUS AND SAINT-ANDRÉ

Dom Placid, Dom Maur's younger brother, became the first abbot of the Belgian abbey of Maredsous which was founded from Beuron. To this monastery belongs the merit of having published the first complete translation of the Missal for the use of the laity, a work which emerged victorious from the controversies on the legitimacy of translating the sacred text of the liturgy and especially that of the canon of the Mass.[3]

It is clear, then, how to the concern for liturgical restoration, referring back to a particular point in tradition, was joined the supplementary concern, acknowledged as fundamental, to bring the liturgy within the reach of the ordinary laity. The archeological tendency was eliminated and Maredsous began the struggle, still going on, to bring the liturgy out from the antiquated framework within which it had been confined and in God's light to set it out before his people.

Thus, a year after the publication of the Missal, during the liturgical congress held at Liège in 1883, Dom Gérard van Caloen read a paper, which attracted some attention and a certain amount of controversy, on the subject of communion during Mass. Subsequently, he founded the first liturgical review, *Le Messager des fidèles*, which afterwards under Dom Germain Morin, a follower of Dom Wolf's and through him of Scheeben's, became *La Revue bénédictine*, a critical and learned organ.

Meanwhile, Maredsous made a foundation at Louvain (Mont-César), which we shall encounter again with Dom

---

[3] It is perhaps worth pointing out that an English translation of the Missal by Dr Husenbeth (1796–1872) antedated the French one by at least half a century. (*Trans.*)

Lambert Beauduin, and Dom Gérard van Caloen established a house at Saint-André, Lophem, near Bruges, which was to achieve considerable development in the liturgical and missionary fields. Here it was that the tradition begun by Dom Gérard was to be perpetuated and reach its full stature; its first phase was the work of Dom Gaspar Lefebvre whose Missal, in many editions and various languages, has sold hundreds of thousands of copies; the second phase came with the review *Paroisse et liturgie* which at the end of the last war developed from the *Bulletin liturgique et paroissial* and at the present moment, with its editorial team under Dom Thierry Maertens, represents the most clearly defined pastoral trend among liturgical reviews in French.

At this point we can conclude this first sketch of the liturgical renewal which issued from monastic sources, leaving mention of the Rhineland abbey of Maria Laach, which has a more direct connection with the achievements of liturgical research, and of Dom Lambert Beauduin, to the starting-point of what in the strict sense of the term is called the "liturgical movement"—that is, as it is based on pastoral work in parishes and the various movements.

Indeed we have already reached this point with Maredsous and Saint-André so that we can conclude this chapter with mention not only of the benefits of the monastic liturgical renewal but also of its limitations.

MERITS AND LIMITATIONS OF THE MONASTIC LITURGICAL MOVEMENT

The great merit of the monastic liturgical movement is that it made a start. In addition, right from the beginning, it brought with it a guarantee of religious authenticity that many of the so called pastoral improvisations are far from possessing. Thus the monasteries preserved and renewed the liturgy at a period when other institutions in the Church did not understand it and would probably have made matters even worse if they had attempted anything in this field.

On the other hand, monasticism shows certain limitations and sometimes the following disadvantages in the matter of liturgy. In the first place, there is the tendency to archeologism, a danger pointed out by Guardini to the bishop of Mainz and by Pius XII in *Mediator*. This danger is to be discerned to some extent with Dom Casel (as we shall see) as well as with the two Wolter brothers or Dom Guéranger. It is to be supposed that the "preservation of ancient monuments" mentality, which is contemporary with the first liturgical restoration, finally spread to this field also. The title of the great dictionary edited by Dom Cabrol and Dom Leclercq (*Dictionnaire d'archéologie chrétienne et de liturgie*) is not without significance in this respect.

Then, there is the tendency to aestheticism of which a famous example is to hand in Huysmans' conception of liturgy which he derived from its presentation in monasteries, or again, Claudel's idea of it, though he is far less monastic, as it is to be seen in *La Messe là-bas*. This tendency is to be clearly seen in the fact which is still usual that the monks celebrate and officiate while the faithful are onlookers. It is even general for it to be forbidden for the laity to sing during a monastic office. And this is not abnormal since the "congregation" in the monastic order of things is formed by the choir of monks alone. But in this case the danger is considerable when this liturgy is put forward as an example to be imitated in parochial liturgies. To cite but one disadvantage, there can be a tendency to make the solemnity of the liturgy consist in its external splendour and its performance by the officiants alone. Now the solemnity of the liturgy resides, as Dom Thierry Maertens has pointed out, in the presence of the people of God taking their own part in the common prayer.

Another limitation of the monastic liturgical renewal comes from the value itself of monastic life. The monk, accustomed to reading the Bible, easily penetrating the full meaning of the prayer, feels no need for the teaching function of the liturgy, the living language and more expressive forms. He is less inclined to recognize the needs of initiation among the faithful, needs that of course are constituent parts of the liturgy which is itself a catechetical initiation, as we shall see below.

For all these reasons the monastic liturgical movement has in the past suffered from the danger of keeping the liturgy as the special preserve of a humanly and religiously cultured caste; this is one of the most serious choices that can be made, quite legitimately of course, by this or that monastic community in which the liturgy is deliberately made to fall into line with forms of life, civilization and culture regarded as classical and ideal but which cannot be considered as invariably applicable to every kind of human group within the Church.

To sum up: the advantages and limitations of the monastic liturgical effort enable us to discern two apparently strongly contrasting laws. The first is that the liturgy is fundamental on the same score as Christianity itself (it is not a workshop open to all), hence the providential rôle of the monasteries as "conservatories" of liturgy. But at the same time the limitations of a monastic presentation of liturgy at the pastoral level are a verification of Fr Jungmann's remark: "Liturgical reform cannot come only from above."

CHAPTER II

LITURGICAL CENTRES, INSTITUTES AND CONFERENCES

In dealing here with the various centres of liturgical research and propaganda we hardly leave the monastic setting with which we have so far been occupied, for this chapter deals principally with certain institutions which have been established in different countries with the help of monks and sometimes also under their direction. But in continuing to follow the pastoral trend of the liturgical movement, which it began to take at Maredsous and Saint-André, we could hardly give here, even in abridged form, the history of the various branches of ecclesiastical science which have contributed to this movement. To do so would have meant following the history and providing a list of all the archeological and literary documents, both in Scripture and patristics, discovered and interpreted by scholars and researchers of the calibre of Duchesne, Andrieu or Bishop.

RESEARCH INSTITUTES

Germany: the school of Maria Laach

The German liturgical movement, as we have already noticed, has its roots in a rediscovery of the Fathers and of ecclesiology, the two great artisans of this work being the theologians Scheeben and Möhler. But beyond all question to the abbey of Maria Laach belongs the honour of having laid the foundations of the modern liturgical movement on a firm doctrinal basis and of having put a varied selection of its practical applications to the proof. Three names stand out in this connection—Dom Ildephonsus Herwegen, Dom Odo Casel and Fr Johannes Pinsk, respectively, abbot, monk and friend of Maria Laach, have made this monastery the centre of liturgical life in the German-speaking countries. (Klosterneuburg in Austria, mentioned below, owes much to Maria Laach and its work is closely connected with it.)

The various movements and institutions depending on Maria Laach can be clearly seen as belonging to two categories; there are those which are concerned principally with the Mystery in liturgy and those which give more attention to anthropology and sociology. Maria Laach forms their inspiration and their principal source at the levels both of doctrine and research; it is for this reason that it has been included in the present chapter.

The principal achievements of the three men mentioned above should be briefly mentioned. Dom Ildephonsus Herwegen (†1948) gave a number of conferences which he afterwards collected together in volume form. He founded a yearbook of liturgy (*Jahrbuch für Liturgiewissenschaft*) and a periodical (*Ecclesia Orans*) together with an academy of patristic studies and a centre for sacred art. But his principal achievement was to get away from the romantic, medieval notion of liturgy that had been current since the work of Dom Guéranger. Dom Herwegen was able to show, to the surprise of many, that the Middle Ages were not, in liturgy at any rate, the Christian era *par excellence*, and that during this period the worship of the Church became overlaid with all sorts of fanciful interpretations, developments foreign to its nature, thus paving the way "for the abandonment of the liturgy by Protestantism and its final disgrace and neglect in so much of post-Tridentine Catholicism".[1]

The *Jahrbuch* founded by Dom Herwegen was carried on

[1] L. Bouyer, *Liturgical Piety*, p. 15.

by Dom Odo Casel (†1948), the most original thinker of the group. He was the author of *Das Christliche Kultmysterium* (1932; English translation referred to in the Select Bibliography), a work which caused some controversy on its first appearance and indeed still continues to do so, though it has also been hailed as the most outstanding theological work of the century. Dom Casel also produced other works on the mystery of feasts and the mystery of the Mass. His teaching is examined below in chapter VI.

Fr Johannes Pinsk was profoundly impressed by the liturgical realism of Maria Laach. After a post as chaplain to students in Berlin he was one of the principal leaders of the *Akadermikerverband* and then parish priest of Lankwitz, Berlin. As editor of a liturgical review, and the author of two books on certain aspects of worship, he exerted a certain influence on the liturgical movement in Germany. His two series of articles, one on the liturgical year and the other on the sociological, anthropological and pastoral conditioning of the liturgy, have been regarded as classics of the liturgical revival.

France: the Centre de Pastorale liturgique

The Centre de Pastorale liturgique (usually referred to as CPL) in France has been compared to the German centre at Maria Laach. It might be objected that this comparison is based on a mistaken classification of the work of the CPL which is thereby effectively denied its pastoral quality and relegated to the category of a research institute. But this classification has been maintained for two reasons: the first is the undeniable high quality of the studies undertaken by the CPL and their extraordinary proliferation; the second is the access that these studies give to the results of scientific research in the field of liturgy—to those matters, in fact, which, as was mentioned at the beginning of this chapter, cannot be dealt with here. Indeed the CPL deserves high praise for the fact that by calling on specialists in all branches of ecclesiastical learning it has been instrumental, both in France and outside it, in preventing the liturgical movement from turning into a series of merely practical prescriptions for liturgical propaganda—a danger, always present, which has not been avoided in some countries, when work of this nature is not based on real research and theological thought. There can hardly be cause for complaint that at the present moment the CPL, despite its numerous public manifestations and the services of a pastoral nature that it renders, appears rather as an academy for liturgical research and thought. This is particularly true since the foundation of the *Institut supérieur de liturgie* at the Institut Catholique in Paris, under the joint direction of the CPL and the abbey of Mont-César, for training seminary professors in this branch.

The present stage of evolution of the CPL was obvious from the beginning, for it started immediately after the war, being founded by two Dominicans, Frs Duployé and Roguet, with Canon Martimort, and sought to group men of learning, theologians and pastors. On the other hand, its legitimate concern to guard against the insubordination of certain unenlightened elements in France, as in Germany, and to give complete assurance to the hierarchy, certainly helped it to maintain itself in the loftier and calmer sphere of ideas and principles. Perhaps it was led thereby, sometimes unconsciously, to discourage other teams which, if less well equipped, were possibly more actively engaged in the pastoral field, by condemning them, practically speaking, to silence.

In any case, as early as 1946 the *Osservctore Romano* bore undeniable witness to the approval that the CPL had obtained at the highest level of ecclesiastical authority and to its general policy. In a laudatory note published on January 17th, 1946, the semi-official journal of the Roman curia emphasized the various indications that led it to believe that the liturgical movement had reached a decisive turning-point of its history and would take the right road; it praised the CPL as being "the consoling and flowering springtime of a Christian spirituality coming from and fed by the pure springs of the *lex orandi*".

Further testimony, if needed, is to be found just ten years

later in the success of the Assisi congress. Although this was not the exclusive work of the CPL it came to the fore as the leader and king-pin of the movement.

Usually the CPL seeks to exert an influence at the parochial level by its public meetings and liturgical weeks and among the Christian public in general through its popular illustrated periodical *Fêtes et Saisons* which has a high circulation. Its permanent activities find their expression in a quarterly review, *La Maison-Dieu*, and the basic works published in the series *Lex Orandi*.

THE LITURGICAL MOVEMENT IN ENGLISH-SPEAKING COUNTRIES

Great Britain and Ireland

Just as it would be wrong to say that there are no signs of a liturgical movement in Great Britain, so it would be to assert that up to the end of the last war this movement had taken a firm hold on the Church in these countries. Certain ideas had penetrated from abroad, but in general they remained at the notional level or were adopted by some as ready-made practical solutions of the liturgical problem, and this occurred in both instances because the necessary preliminary theological thinking and liturgical research had been done by others and was not the product of native effort. An authentic movement requires some at least of the preliminary spadework to be done on the spot and not to be left to the scholars and liturgists of other countries.

Nevertheless, as appears later in this section, there are signs of much improvement. Of course, there were several reasons for the tardy start of the liturgical movement in Great Britain, reasons which go back to the nineteenth century and beyond to the time of persecution.

The historical position emerges plainly from such a book as Dom Rousseau's *Progress of the Liturgy* where of the twenty short pages devoted to England (the restriction to the one country is Dom Rousseau's) all but three of them are concerned with Anglicans. There can be no quarrel with this for it represents accurately enough the real position: a little over a hundred years ago Anglicans—or at least that portion of them actively concerned with the Oxford movement—were occupied in those tasks of *ressourcement* which we nowadays realize to be of capital importance, while the Catholics, emerging from a period of persecution, with very different problems on their hands (for example, the influx of poor Irish due to the famine, the difficulties inherent in the re-establishment of the hierarchy in 1850, lack of financial resources, etc.) though benefiting in some degree from the research done by Anglicans were largely preoccupied with other matters.

It has also to be borne in mind that though the Catholics were doctrinally the heirs to the pre-Reformation Church in England, professing the same faith and using the same liturgy as their forefathers, what can only be called the ethos of the pre-Reformation Church seemed to have lingered on among certain sections of Anglicanism. For this reason many converts to Catholicism, endeavouring to make a clean break with their immediate religious past, identified themselves with an expression of Catholicism as it was to be found in some parts of Italy in the nineteenth century, and adopted various devotional practices which, while no doubt picturesque among the Italian peasants where they evolved, were out of place in England and out of tune with the English religious mind. Fr Faber was an obvious example of such a reaction.

The influences at work in Germany and France were not without their impact in England. Dom Rousseau points out that there is a certain affinity between Newman and Möhler and he quotes Fr de Grandmaison's remark that "if in the iron age of theology constituted by the first three-quarters of the nineteenth century a name of destiny and enduring renown is sought, the first to appear is Möhler's, standing almost alone with Newman's". Newman frequently quotes Möhler and liked to regard him as his precursor. Neither of them was directly concerned with liturgy but the connection between them for what concerns us here is to be found in their love of Christian antiquity and the Fathers and in their appeal to them in their efforts to rechristianize their own period.

Dom Guéranger, too, was not without influence since his *Liturgical Year* appeared in translation soon after its original publication; this was the work of Dom Laurence Shepherd. But the same forces were at work in England as in France; as a rule any attempt at liturgical restoration went hand in hand with the "Gothic revival" in architecture and was conceived in terms of a return to the Middle Ages; most of the work done among Catholics was merely rubrical or else strictly historical. Dr Husenbeth, as has already been mentioned, translated the Missal; Dr Daniel Rock (1799–1871), a priest esteemed by his contemporaries for his learning, produced a treatise on the liturgy of the Mass that went through several editions: *Hierugia, or the Holy Sacrifice of the Mass* (London, 1833). He also produced a three-volume work on the Sarum rite and its ordinary, attributed in those days to St Osmund. But all this was largely archeology rather than what we are concerned with here.

Nevertheless, Dr Rock's work, like Dr Husenbeth's Missal, is symptomatic of a frame of mind and an approach to the liturgy of the Church that differed considerably from the type of worship that was introduced by, for example, the Oratorians in London in the middle of the nineteenth century. Husenbeth and Rock both belonged to the old English Catholic tradition which is also exemplified by Bishop Challoner's *Garden of the Soul*. This popular prayerbook, which has run through so many editions that it is probably impossible now to enumerate them all, has, unfortunately, been almost edited out of recognition. In its original form it contained a wealth of material from the worship of the Church, psalms and hymns and the like, that is now no longer included. The same tradition is revealed by the earlier volumes of the *Catholic Directory*, or the later volumes of the *Laity's Catholic Directory*; therein it may be discovered that High Mass and Vespers of a Sunday were the usual church services provided for Catholics in London in, say,

1829, and that the number of churches with Sunday Vespers then was far greater than it is today. Moreover, there were books in print which provided the laity with the text of this Office in their own language as well as in Latin.

But practically speaking the romantic medieval attitude towards liturgy, or else the rubrical approach, prevailed in Great Britain until well on into the twentieth century and it was only after the First World War that the real implications of the liturgical revival at the parochial level gained gradual recognition. Even so this realization was confined to a small number of clergy and laity. With the publication of *Mediator* (1947) and subsequent decrees, the reform of the Holy Week services, the directives about dialogue Mass, gradually a different mentality has begun to emerge among the younger clergy, but in the absence of clear leadership and encouragement from the bishops progress has necessarily been slow. That was the position prior to the Liturgical Constitution of the Second Vatican Council; this has given an entirely new perspective to the whole liturgical question in the British Isles.

Yet it is not true to say that, generally speaking, there has been little progress. Judged by the standard of even twenty years ago progress has been enormous. Before the Council dialogue Mass was widespread and real efforts were being made in some places to make the worship of the Church a living reality. Then the publication of books like Fr Charles Davis's *Liturgy and Doctrine*, which is fundamental, is just one symptom of the kind of work being done; in this book the theological revival and the liturgical revival are all linked together, showing the fundamental nature of the latter. It is a good example of the kind of theological preparation needed for an authentic liturgical movement. Of course, there have been many translations from the French and German, and it is good for English-speaking people thus to be in touch with thought in Europe, but translations rarely have the impact of a book which has been thought out in the language in which it is presented to readers, and which confronts a concrete situation in the experience of authors and readers alike.

The Society of St Gregory, founded between the wars with a predominant interest in plainchant, after the Second World War enlarged its scope to promote the liturgical revival in accordance with the principles laid down in *Mediator*. Its periodical *Liturgy* (formerly *Music and Liturgy*), ably edited by Fr J. D. Crichton, now publishes informative and valuable material and contrives to keep readers in touch with developments elsewhere; by means of its summer and other "schools" the Society of St Gregory has done much useful work. The Vernacular Society exists for the purpose indicated by its name; it is not widely supported but it has possibly exerted an influence in excess of its membership. Certainly, the symposium that it sponsored (*English in the Liturgy*, edited by C. R. A. Cunliffe, London, 1956) aroused considerable comment. Now that its principal purpose has been achieved it could usefully devote its energies to other work in the liturgical field.

In Ireland a beginning has been made in post-war years with the annual conferences for clergy held at Glenstal Abbey. Much has been done in recent years to promote a more realistic attitude towards the liturgical movement by the monthly review *The Furrow*; edited from Maynooth, a fact not without importance, since here a great number of the clergy who are to work in Ireland are trained, it has wisely not confined itself to liturgy, but has been concerned with the whole problem of the presentation of Christianity to the modern world. Certainly all the signs are that if the liturgical movement has begun to exert an influence in Ireland at a late stage in its development it has at least started on the right lines and with an entirely pastoral outlook, thus avoiding the mistakes made elsewhere.

Evidence for this is to be found in the *Collectio Rituum* published in 1960. This bilingual ritual for use in all the dioceses of Ireland is not just a reprint of the Roman Ritual with a translation of certain of its rites; the opportunity has been taken to revise some of the rites in order to make them better suited to conditions prevailing in Ireland at the present time. In this respect the Irish bilingual Ritual compares very favourably with the *Excerpta e Rituali* published at about the same time for use in England and Wales; in this no attempt has been made at adaptation and the book contains a straightforward translation of certain portions of the Roman Ritual.

Since 1954 an annual liturgical congress has been held in Ireland at Glenstal Abbey the papers of which have been published in two volumes (*Studies in Pastoral Liturgy*, I and II); these reveal very clearly that those taking part are very much alive to the problems of Christian worship in modern times and to the danger of taking over ready made the solutions arrived at elsewhere. The Editor of the latest volume of *Studies in Pastoral Liturgy* puts this very clearly:

> Obviously we have much to learn in Ireland from countries where the liturgical movement can be traced back to the beginning of this century; it would be, nonetheless, an unwise policy simply to transpose to this country practices in vogue on the continent and to impose them on our people—a policy of eclecticism which would be assured of no lasting results. We must work out our own solutions in the light of the Church's teaching, liturgical tradition and pastoral experience.[2]

All the signs are, then, that the liturgical movement in Ireland made a start which though late was healthy.

The United States

In the United States the liturgical revival owes its origins and much of its later development to the Benedictine monks of St John's Abbey, Collegeville, Minnesota. Indeed, more than anywhere else, the introduction of the revival to the U.S.A. was the work of one man, Dom Virgil Michel. His efforts

> had effects on the life of the Church throughout the whole of the United States and in varying degrees throughout the English-speaking world. For in the mid-1920's an organized movement was brought from Europe and launched at St John's by Michel with the support of his abbot which Theodore Maynard in his *Story of American Catholicism* has termed the most significant

[2] *Studies in Pastoral Liturgy*, II, p. viii.

aspect of contemporary religious life. It is called the liturgical movement, or more correctly the liturgical revival.[3]

The actual birth of the movement may be said to have taken place with the publication of the first number of *Orate Fratres* under Dom Virgil Michel's editorship in Advent, 1925. It is significant that Dom Virgil combined liturgical knowledge with an active social concern; his inauguration of the movement therefore avoided many of the pitfalls encountered elsewhere. *Orate Fratres* (which changed its name to the more appropriate *Worship* after the Second World War) has continued to make progress. From the Liturgical Day, held at St John's Abbey in 1929, to the first national Liturgical Week, under Benedictine sponsorship, in 1940, progress has not been slow. Certain names stand out: Fr Godfrey Diekmann, O.S.B., successor to Fr Virgil Michel as editor of *Orate Fratres* (*Worship*), in 1963 completed twenty-five years service in that position. During this period Fr Godfrey Diekmann has unquestionably been one of the most prominent and influential figures in the American liturgical movement. He is now vice-president of the Liturgical Conference and is acting as *peritus* on the liturgy commission of the Second Vatican Council. Fr Gerard Ellard was another pioneer. From the time that he began writing in 1923 until his sudden death in 1963, Fr Ellard contributed steadily to the liturgical apostolate through his numerous books and articles, both popular and scholarly, through his numerous lectures throughout the country and through his many years as a teacher. Fr Michael Mathis, C.S.C., was another significant figure in the American movement. Perhaps his best known contribution is the founding of the Summer School of Liturgy at the University of Notre Dame.

In recent years the most influential figure has been Fr Frederick R. McManus, J.C.D., a professor of canon law at the Catholic University at Washington, a *peritus* on the liturgy commission of the Second Vatican Council. His books, his

[3] Colman J. Barry, O.S.B., *Worship and Work* (Collegeville, Minn., 1956), p. 264.

monthly column in *Worship*, his numerous lectures and his work as President of the Liturgical Conference have established him as an international authority on liturgy. Other outstanding names are Mgr Hellriegel and the late Fr Laukemper with their work for the promotion of liturgical life as the normal manifestation of the parish and Fr Rheinhold with his lively and well-informed articles and books.

A recent survey has indicated that something like sixty per cent of the 140 dioceses in the United States have set up liturgical commissions, and although it is impossible to provide an accurate figure on the number of parishes in which the congregation participates actively in the Mass, it is certainly safe to say that there is some degree of active participation in more than half the parishes of the country.

Thus there are signs that the fundamental ideas of the liturgical movement have made considerable progress among the Catholics of the U.S.A. In addition the publication and authorization of the bilingual Ritual in 1954, five years before the jejune compilation authorized for England and Wales, showed that the Church authorities were alive to the problems of the day. This book, containing revisions of some of the rites, was probably the best of the bilingual Rituals in the English-speaking world, and closely rivalled its German counterpart in excellence. Unfortunately, the second edition, published in 1961, authorized far less English than the previous edition.

The first national Liturgical Week was held in 1940 under the sponsorship of the Benedictine Liturgical Conference and the Week has been held annually ever since. At the twenty-fourth Week, held in August 1963, there were fourteen thousand registrants who filled the Convention Hall in Philadelphia —significant progress since the first meeting held in the basement of the cathedral in Chicago. In 1943 it was decided that the Benedictine Liturgical Conference should be dissolved in favour of a more representative organization; in 1944 it was reconstituted and incorporated as The Liturgical Conference.

The liturgical revival in the United States was indeed fortunate in its founder. After Dom Virgil's early death in 1938, Fr H. A. Rheinhold wrote:

> It is almost beyond human comprehension to grasp the completeness with which he absorbed everything that Austria, Belgium and Germany had to offer. But greater yet was what he did with it. Instead of dragging his find across the border as an exotic museum piece, he made it American as only an American mind can make it. He had seen the high sweep of German ecclesiology and sacramentalism; he had admired the Belgians for their clear grasp of a new spirituality and their critical awareness of all that stood in the way of liturgical ecclesiastical piety from traditional carry-overs; he had learned in Austria what the common people could gather from the Church's treasures without fright, but he did not come back to force these foreign and incoherent moulds on the American Church. Besides, his clear realism and his burning apostle's heart had one urge none of the great masters in Europe seemed to see; the connection of social justice with a new social spirituality. For Virgil Michel the labour encyclicals of Leo XIII and the liturgical reforms of Pius X did not just by accident happen within one generation, but were responses to cries of the masses for Christ, who had power and gave the good tidings. They belonged together.[4]

EUROPEAN COUNTRIES OTHER THAN FRANCE AND GERMANY

It can hardly be said that the liturgical movement has made great strides in Spain, Italy and Portugal. In Spain the liturgical renewal is promoted principally by the Benedictine abbey of Montserrat in Catalonia, which is a well-known centre not only of pilgrimage but also of liturgical worship and of the publication of books popularizing the fundamental ideas of the liturgical movement. There should also be mentioned the abbey of San Domingo de Los Silos in the province of Burgos which publishes a review *Liturgia*. Since 1954 annual congresses of pastoral liturgy have been organized and less intermittent activity has been pursued in the seminaries. In 1955 a

---

[4] *National Liturgical Week Proceedings* (1947), p. 11.

central committee for the liturgical apostolate was set up in Toledo.

In Italy, to the extent that liturgical progress can be distinguished from directions given by Rome, there may be mentioned the existence of the *Centro di Azione liturgica* which publishes a *Rivista liturgica*; once again this is a Benedictine work since it is published by the Abbey of Finalpia in the province of Savona; here too is organized an annual liturgical congress. It is worth pointing out, also, the connection between the work of Cardinal Schuster, a Benedictine monk who became archbishop of Milan, and that at the present day of Cardinal Lercaro, archbishop of Bologna. The works of both are certainly typical of their respective generations. Thus it is interesting to observe how the period of research as represented by Cardinal Schuster's work has led to that of a pastoral approach, intelligently open to the data of sociology. The particular significance of Cardinal Schuster's work in connection with the Italian liturgical movement since its origins is emphasized below.

CONCLUSION

At the end of this chapter, devoted to the various centres of research and propaganda in the sphere of pastoral liturgy, an attempt may be made to classify the various branches of the ecclesiastical sciences employed by workers in the field, whether scholars or pastors, who have combined in the liturgical movement learning and piety. There is nothing original about this since right at the beginning of the century a monk of Solesmes, Dom Aubourg, portrayed in the *Revue Grégorienne* his conception of the ideal liturgist. The following extracts are offered for the entertainment as well as for the edification of the reader:

> The scientific equipment of the ideal liturgist should comprise at least the following: a good general education, a solid theological foundation, five or six ancient languages, and the same number of modern ones. . . . And those are only the preliminary requirements. The threefold face of antiquity—Semitic, Greek

and Latin—will be familiar to him. He should possess a thorough knowledge of the political history of the Middle Ages and an equally thorough knowledge of the history of the Church, of her dogmas and her discipline. . . . Set your mind at rest, we are only at the beginning. The liturgist's own particular task begins with the study of the liturgical texts, the texts of all the liturgies, which he must submit to painstaking analysis and continual comparison. From the data that he thus extracts from them he will be able to construct a doctrine of the liturgy or to retrace its history. . . . But this is only the stage of accumulating materials. The final work consists in the fusion of doctrine and history in a synthesis which should make clear to men's minds the gradual development of the first seeds of the Christian mysteries in the infinite frondescence of liturgical rites.

This passage, which is not without its exaggerations, can be summarized in a less colourful manner. The principal branches of learning, which in actual fact have been utilized in liturgy, are the following:

In the first place, history and archeology, particularly in connection with the Bible and the patristic and medieval periods, and even to such an extent that Pius XII was obliged to utter a warning against an excessive and unhealthy pre-occupation with things of the past, declaring that it would be "neither wise nor praiseworthy to reduce everything to antiquity by every possible device" (*Mediator*). On the other hand, these branches of learning are especially allied with liturgy, which is essentially conservative, by its unchanging character expressing in some sort a sign of transcendence and instinctively resistant to any kind of fanciful innovation as well as to any unjustified modification.

Secondly comes ecclesiastical law, in its various aspects, but specifically as liturgical law, on a final analysis degenerating into knowledge of rubrics: just as with "archeologism", it is almost superfluous to protest against such a debased and narrow view of the subject.

Then, there is theology, and especially ecclesiology. Indeed, it seems almost commonplace now to point out a genetic development occurring between ecclesiology, derived from its biblical and patristic sources, and the liturgical movement.

Finally there is a branch of knowledge, which while being an art and not a science in the proper sense of the word, appears to be most important of all: this is the pastoral aspect. The title of Fr Jungmann's paper at the Assisi congress in 1956 was significant in this respect: "Pastoral care, the key to the history of the liturgy." It can be said that it was pastoral needs which brought the liturgical forms into being in the primitive Church: and so it is this which enables us to discover the reason for the liturgical forms of the past and which can devise forms adapted to the present needs of the faithful. The truth of this emerges clearly from the whole effort of liturgical catechesis and it can be seen, too, in the fact that in Pius XII's liturgical reforms the principal motivation was to be found generally in pastoral reasons.

But all this brings us into the perspective of other sciences which until a few years ago were still wholly unknown to the pastoral clergy. These are the auxiliary sciences, mostly of a clearly secular character, which nevertheless prove as necessary as the so-called ecclesiastical sciences. In passing, we can mention, for example, ethnology and the history of religions, sociology and individual and crowd psychology. This short list is indicative that pastoral liturgy, if it is not to be merely imitative of the past, even of a golden age for the Church, or, with greater reason, merely a matter of innovation, must enlarge its views to embrace the whole religious world in order to obtain a certain number of fundamental ideas and especially the laws and, so to say, the constants of the individual and collective religious mind. For it is these that it is important to promote in the present conditions of societies and their respective civilizations.

CHAPTER III

PAROCHIAL DEVELOPMENTS

The views touched on at the end of the last chapter in connection with the social and cultural evolution of the contemporary world, together with its religious diversity, scarcely suspected, it seems, by Christians, should not discourage us from returning to consideration of more modest matters. In these, indeed, can be discerned the authentic effects of the liturgical movement at the present time.

As an introduction to this chapter we can consider a further piece of history which might well have found a place at the beginning of either of the preceding chapters or serve as a summary of the whole volume. This is the outstanding work of Dom Lambert Beauduin.

DOM LAMBERT BEAUDUIN

It is fitting and right that just a few years after his death a short account of Dom Lambert Beauduin's work should appear at the head of these few remarks on the parochial development of the liturgical movement. The liturgy is rightfully the worship of the Christian people: but in fact it is due to Dom Lambert Beauduin that its pastoral dimensions have been discovered in the present renewal. Many others after him, and some even before him, worked on the same lines. But beyond all question to him belongs the credit for the primary intuition, even to the extent that it is possible to date the liturgical movement in the proper sense of the term from the first expression that he gave to this intuition in 1909. It has been said indeed that "Dom Beauduin's intuitions form, no doubt, the principal characteristic of his genius".

But if that is true it is important to consider his thought on the pastoral implications of the liturgy in conjunction with two other intuitions of his without which it would lose much of its value. Yet it is on account of these further intuitions that Dom Beauduin is indeed the patriarch and patron of all workers in this field, whatever their special interest in it.

Dom Lambert Beauduin's view on the pastoral implications of the liturgy (he was a former parish priest and workers' chaplain), through which he gave fresh impetus to the liturgical movement, must be taken in conjunction with his attitude to the Eastern Church in general and Eastern liturgies in particular. In this field he became the leader of a school, and his work was continued, in the face of great difficulties, it must be acknowledged, in particular by the Benedictines of Amay-sur-Meuse, subsequently established at Chevetogne.

The same pastoral approach to the liturgy must be acknowledged as the basis of the scientific and learned work through which Dom Beauduin was effectively aided at Mont-César by the review *Questions liturgiques et paroissiales* and especially by Dom Capelle and Dom Botte.

Having thus delineated Dom Beauduin's fundamental attitudes we can recall some of the facts of the story and its subsequent developments. The origin of the liturgical movement, then, is to be found in 1909 at the Catholic Congress at Malines, in a paper by Dom Lambert Beauduin which earned the support of Cardinal Mercier. On July 7th, 1910 a report was sent by Mont-César to the abbot of Beuron suggesting the setting up of a school of liturgy at Louvain. This report was based on the following premises: liturgical renewal is necessary, it can be directed by the Benedictines and Mont-César seems indicated as the appropriate centre.

At that time, indeed, Dom Beauduin had in mind the holding of liturgical "weeks" (these were later held at the rate of two a year), the establishment of a liturgical review (this was achieved with the founding of *Questions liturgiques et paroissiales*) and finally the founding of a liturgical institute; this unfortunately proved impossible at that time.

In this way the principal characteristics of the liturgical movement of the abbey of Mont-César were that it was brought up to date and adapted to social requirements in all its bearings; as a consequence, its influence was felt far and wide and it found imitators in all countries.

So far as Belgium was concerned Dom Beauduin's liturgical work can be summed up in the threefold aspect which it assumed, corresponding at all points with the trend of the work at Saint-André (referred to above, p. 14). In the first place liturgy is for the service of the parishes, as they are; then, the liturgical renewal is the centre and also the starting-point of a complete parochial renewal; lastly, an attempt must be made to use what we already have; in the light of this experience reform can be effected; there must be neither rigid conservatism nor irresponsible innovation; the primary need is that an attempt should be made.

It was on account of this threefold aspect that this section on Dom Beauduin was placed at the head of the subject which is now to be treated—the liturgical renewal coming out from the monasteries and specialized centres to influence the parishes and popular movements. Germany, where the movement developed especially between the two wars, is here given special mention, followed by France, where the principal expansion took place after World War II. But to begin with some information is offered about the movement at Klosterneuburg in Austria because of its extensive influence and the sympathetic character of the work which was undertaken modestly but methodically in the simple setting of a parish church.

AUSTRIA: THE MOVEMENT AT KLOSTERNEUBURG

The school of Maria Laach, somewhat aristocratic and erudite, had evolved a theology of the liturgy in the tradition of the Fathers and through it influenced an intellectual élite among the faithful. Pius Parsch and his closest collaborator, Joseph Casper, a priest of the Byzantine rite, basing themselves on the principles of Maria Laach, were concerned particularly by what they called *Volksliturgie*, a tautological term perhaps, but one which clearly expresses the fact that liturgy is the people's work, the people's affair.

Yet what is striking at first in the Klosterneuburg movement, a parochial undertaking, is the solid nature of the organization. The basis of it is a publishing company (*Volksliturgische Apostolat*) which forms the financial and administrative side. This company is responsible for a review, *Bibel und Liturgie*, and a remarkable series of the liturgical propers for each week ("Life with the Church"), manuals of all sorts, editions of texts and pictures.

The purpose of one organization was the apostolate among the faithful through the liturgy. Now there are two ways of being concerned with the liturgy. It can be considered in itself, its origins and its symbolism studied, an attempt can be made to arrive at absolute purity of text and rite and to establish the authentic rubrics. That is the purpose of the various specialized institutes. Or the faithful can be brought back to an understanding of the liturgy to enable them thus to understand the ceremonies and to return to the ultimate source of authentic prayer. The Klosterneuburg movement was concerned with this latter way of regarding the liturgy.

In the first place it envisaged the restoration of the Mass to its true place and its true meaning—a sacrifice offered by the community and a sacrificial meal. For this purpose was developed a form of preaching directly inspired by the liturgy and evening services were restored to a place of esteem. By evening services were meant the singing of psalms, Compline, Bible reading, ceremonies during which the whole parochial family really takes part in the liturgy. But an important though modest preliminary is to have a proper care for the dignity of the sanctuary; everything in it should contribute to make the altar stand out for it is the place of sacrifice and the centre of liturgical unity.

The chief inspiration of this movement was certainly Dom Pius Parsch, a canon regular of Klosterneuburg. He was ill at ease in the great abbey church (a romanesque church which underwent restoration at the Baroque period) but he managed to restore as the parish church a magnificent little romanesque church dedicated to St Gertrude and situated a few hundred yards from the monastery. It was this church which was referred to in the remark: "The movement became a powerful ferment with enormous influence on parishes and religious communities."

THE MOVEMENT IN GERMANY

The history of the German liturgical movement can be divided conveniently into three stages—the first between 1918 and 1933, the second corresponding to the period of National Socialism and the Second World War, and the third stage after the war.

The first stage which drew its inspiration equally from Klosterneuburg and Maria Laach, and corresponds therefore with the development of frequent communion (under the form of monthly communion), is characterized principally by the return of youth to Christian sources hitherto ignored. Here Guardini's rôle was preponderant: "It was perhaps the first time for centuries that an author who was theologian, philosopher, artist and man of letters, embodying the whole living culture of his times, could be so cordially received." In addition to Guardini there should be mentioned several youth movements and also Mgr Volker who was the first to introduce dialogue Mass.

When the Nazis came to power the Church was deprived of all means of external action and was obliged to fall back on her own internal life. This was almost providential for the altar became the centre of Christians' lives and they began to feel that they were back in the period of the primitive Church. At this time the Oratorians at Leipzig and afterwards at Munich undertook their well-known work in the liturgical field. In addition, the important work done by military chaplains should be emphasized.

On obtaining her freedom again the Church was faced with the problem of the direction her activities should take; was she to base everything on the parish? Would she rediscover her former organizations? In point of fact these latter re-appeared, together with others like the Young Christian Workers. But there seemed to be a certain paralysis of the liturgical movement. It was to continue at the scientific level under the direction of Maria Laach, but the movement continued to make its way with varying fortunes and at the mercy of more or less serious incidents under the leadership of the episcopate and the impetus given by two congresses.

In 1920 the bishop of Passau proposed at Fulda that an episcopal commission should be set up with a sub-committee of specialists (Jungmann, Kahlefeld, etc.). The commission was established and an Institute of Liturgy was founded at Trier.

Since 1943 four categories of eucharistic celebration are to be found in Germany. These are *Gemeinschaftmesse* (dialogue Mass), *Bet-undsangmesse* (Mass accompanied with prayers and hymns), *Hochmesse* (high Mass in plainchant, somewhat un-usual in Germany) and *Deutschehochmesse* (German high Mass in which the ordinary is sung in German). This German high Mass was authorized by Rome in 1950 for all German-speaking-countries.

Two congresses took place, at Frankfurt (1950) and at Munich (1955). The first concluded with a resolution calling for the continuance of evening Mass on weekdays, mitigation of the eucharistic fast, and the reading of the lessons at Mass to be in German. The second congress, at which two thousand people took part, was concerned with the important problem of liturgy and personal piety. Two resolutions were passed, the first asking for the reform of all the Holy Week services, the second for the direct reading of the lessons at Mass by the priest in German.

A further step was taken officially. This was the publication of a new catechism bearing a very pronounced liturgical and scriptural stamp and the issue of a new collection of hymns and chants better adapted to the requirements of the liturgy. Lastly, in 1955, came the German ritual. By this time dialogue Masses were in use everywhere. Guardini's translation of the psalms was recommended by the bishops. The new Easter liturgy encountered considerable success and, it is important to note, new churches were built in accordance with the requirements of the liturgical renewal.

Yet clear-sighted priests were seriously concerned. They could observe that, generally speaking, from the liturgical point of view there was a kind of paralysis. For most people, liturgy meant something for show, it did not affect daily life. Does the language of the psalms, they asked, have any meaning for modern man? Sociological conditions at the present day make the liturgical assembly of the faithful difficult. In the provinces there are great numbers of those who are on the threshold of the faith, but the liturgy ought to be the gathering together of the *plebs sancta*. These preoccupations formed the inspiration of the following propositions, about which it can be said general unanimity was achieved.

There can be no question of "archeologism". The liturgy, therefore, must be authentic. Sacred Scripture must have its full and proper place in liturgy. The relationship of liturgy and personal piety must be made clear (allowance must be made for times of silence). The relationship between liturgy and life are equally in need of emphasis; liturgy must be an expression of life. In connection with the liturgical language Kahlefeld proposed that a trial should be made of Gregorian chant to German words for the proper of the Mass; this was not allowed by Rome at the time. It remains to be seen how, after the Second Vatican Council, the liturgical reform which it promulgated will take effect in Germany.

THE MOVEMENT IN FRANCE

"The new phenomenon is that with St Pius X the liturgical movement was freed from the restricted circles of the previous

generation and returned to its own field which is the parish."
Fr Doncoeur, the author of these lines, was himself one of the
intrepid workers in achieving this successful return. We can
see now how at his instigation it was primarily in the youth
movements and the specialized groups that this return
occurred.

Another promoter of the French liturgical renewal, Fr
Bouyer, the occasional acidity of whose criticism is compen-
sated for by his humour, offers us the following account:

> How did our liturgical movement begin? It is difficult to say
> exactly, but it seems that the beginning can be found in the
> youth movements connected in some sort with Catholic Action.
> The Scout movement in the first place was influential here both
> by the kind of liturgical life that it required and by the re-
> actions that it provoked in those that it had trained. ... At the
> material level it seems difficult to imagine how all the accessories
> for benediction of the Blessed Sacrament could be packed up in
> a haversack. Thus for many the Roman Mass began to re-
> appear in all its stark simplicity and vigour. Around an altar,
> which in the nature of things was without gradines, reredos,
> vases or those long sham candles, and in the absence of all
> those "devotional" objects which, though washable in warm
> water cannot, thank God, be carried about, these young men
> rediscovered that the celebration of Mass was a eucharistic
> sacrificial meal.[1]

This amusing account may afford us the occasion to express
if not reproaches at least a certain regret. For if the liturgical
movement rapidly had effect among certain youth movements
and, through them, the parishes, its backwardness, or even its
non-existence, is to be deplored in a great number of institutes
and colleges under the direction of religious, clerics or nuns.
In any case, there are far too many of these places where the
religious exercises could not be better calculated to disgust
(the word is not too strong) the students for the rest of their
lives with every manifestation of religion. Timetables and cere-

[1] L. Bouyer, "Réflexions sur le mouvement liturgique", in *Dieu
Vivant* 19, 85.

monies, usually obligatory, combine together to make the children's practice of religion a sort of nightmare. It is a very great pity that, despite the liturgical renewal, some of the things that we can remember from our schooldays are still to be found today.

Now this is deplorable in two ways. For not only should religious institutions be in a position to celebrate a "living liturgy" more easily than elsewhere but also with the help of well-trained teams they ought to help less-favoured centres. This is what has been done by one Belgian institution in which, instead of sending the children home during Holy Week, or keeping them within the four walls of the school, sent properly trained teams to help neighbouring parishes with the ceremonies of the Easter triduum. If this festival falls at a date inconvenient to scholastic requirements there are nevertheless many similar occasions during the year.

What has been suggested in regard to schools might well be applicable and fruitful *a fortiori* with elder groups, particularly university and other students. It is certainly excellent and attractive to encourage numbers of them to set off on pilgrimage, and it is easy enough to do. On the other hand, how many groups assume adult responsibility in respect of the liturgical renewal by endeavouring to achieve a real insertion of the student element into adult communities?

At the parochial level, after 1920, side by side with the youth movements a few sporadic attempts were made in certain parishes. Canon Rémilleux, parish priest of Saint-Alban in Lyons, was the forerunner of them all. He went to Germany to study and lived for a time in Austria. He regarded Pius Parsch as his great master. Rémilleux's fundamental conception was to establish his parish as a praying community. Four points in this programme need emphasizing: an extraordinary sense of Christian charity; the one centre of the parish is the altar; the sacraments are the occasion of bringing to the liturgy those who only occasionally come to church; there is no authentic liturgy without a very thorough biblical formation.

Following Canon Rémilleux's example various parishes took

steps to place the liturgical renewal in the forefront of their pastoral preoccupations. To take two examples from among many, Mgr Chevrot at Saint-François-Xavier in Paris was well known, and in the dechristianized Parisian suburbs the Benedictine parish of Hay-les-Roses makes the liturgy the centre of its pastoral activity.

After Mgr Chevrot (†1958) a different style appears. In this case it is not a question of liturgy and still less of preaching. Liturgical pastoral methods are entirely integrated into a more comprehensive conception of the specifically missionary character of a Christian community, which ought to have no other reason for its existence. The classical formulation of this truth, which ought to be self-evident after the revelation of *France Pagan?*, was given in Abbé Michonneau's *The Missionary Spirit in Parish Life* (1952).

The situation has so far evolved that one can no longer speak of pastoral liturgy. The expression has become too narrow. Pastoral liturgy is only one element in missionary pastoral methods or, better still, in catechumenal pastoral methods. For if the first stage of the parochial liturgical movement consists in transforming the parish, by means of the liturgical renewal in particular, beginning with an administrative organization (civil parish, district, etc.) into a living community (first stage), and within this community of prayer and charity there grows up an awareness of missionary needs (second stage), the third and last stage still awaiting the renewed parish is a complete reconstruction bringing it back to its primary purpose which is the incorporation of new adult members by means of the catechumenate. The stages are, then, from administration to living community, from living community to missionary community, and from the latter to catechumenal community.

This is what a group of parishes in Paris and the provinces have endeavoured to achieve and to formulate in the review *Paroisse et Mission* with its counterpart in the series *Mission et Sociologie*. The purpose, among others, of these publications is to prevent the feeling of self-satisfaction when some small advance has been made liturgically, and to integrate liturgical endeavour in the general work of the apostolate without depriving worship in normally constituted communities of its place as the starting-point and as the end of the apostolate. Of course there is no question of confusing everything together, nor of sacrificing anything, but rather of distinguishing clearly the various functions in the Christian community and of subordinating them hierarchically in the conscience and in the practice of pastors and the laity concerned. Now a part of the present generation has perhaps been too exclusively concerned with the liturgical renewal (though the greater part of this generation has not yet awakened to the fact of the liturgical renewal, when, that is, it does not despise or oppose those who are alive to it). At present it is a matter of so acting that the liturgical movement as a whole assumes a missionary aspect (if it does not it will wither away) and that the missionary movement brings about a return to an authentically renewed liturgy, a "catechumenal" liturgy, as it really was in the springtime of the Church. It was already a great step forward when the liturgical movement passed from the monasteries into the parishes, but it still remains a talent buried in the ground if its place in the whole scheme of the Christian witness of the ecclesiastical community is not given proper emphasis. And this community will, or will not, be catechumenal.

At this point we come directly to the points raised by Mgr van Bekkum, Bishop of Ruteng (Flores, Indonesia), at the Assisi congress. He was speaking, of course, of pagan peoples in missionary countries in the proper sense of the term.

Having shown that with the emerging Afro-Asiatic nations a solely western liturgy would rightly or wrongly revive hostility to foreign influences and that pagan devotional worship should be considered as a preparation for Christian worship (complete abolition of all pagan forms of worship and the substitution of skimped and incomprehensible low Masses results in a devitalization of converts' piety) the missionary bishop went on to show that, of its very nature, the liturgy, although it includes, of course, the proclamation of the Word in the Christian community, in the face of the pagan world is missionary by right. That may be a banal observation for many pastors for whom authentic rites and ceremonies, well carried out, form a privileged means of reaching unbelievers at a genuinely religious level. And so it would be wrong to put "liturgy" on one side and "mission" on the other.

To return to the present state of French Catholicism which, unlike that of other countries, particularly England and Ireland, comprises a minority of practising Catholics among a mass of those who call themselves believers and do not practise (and who probably have never had the faith preached to them): in these circumstances pastoral liturgy and missionary work should in many cases be closely entwined—the liturgy of the dead, baptism, first communion, instructions to engaged couples, marriage (at the present time this sacrament corresponds to baptism administered to adults in the primitive Church), the teaching given at the great Christian festivals to the practising Catholics, and to the others also because these recurrent occasions of the year have passed into popular folklore, all these offer innumerable opportunities for pastoral initiative of the first importance. It is on these frequent occasions that Canon Martimort's words find complete verification: "It seems quite clear nowadays that liturgy and evangelization far from being contradictory are two complementary functions which must both be accomplished without the right of choosing between them or of opposing one to the other."

Liturgy, therefore, is missionary in so far as it is initiation, but there are certain limitations in fact and in law where evangelization is concerned. For liturgy is only really authentic for those who are initiated, for those, that is, who have been awakened to the whole faith by the Word of God and by catechumenal contact with the Christian community. It encounters the same limitations as the parish which under the present territorial organization does not always reach people where they are.

For these reasons, in addition to the urgency of the reconstruction of the parochial system, we have emphasized also the reconversion of the liturgical movement which, if it is true that it fulfils its aim in the parishes, with them runs the danger, nevertheless, of becoming ineffective. At the end of this short historical sketch of the liturgical renewal it was important to show in this way that the story has not yet come to an end; indeed it has only just begun.

THE RÔLE OF THE BISHOPS

In many cases the liturgical renewal at the parochial level has been given a certain impulsion by the bishop at the diocesan level—diocesan liturgical sessions and congresses, episcopal regulations and pastoral letters have revealed the increasing interest of the bishops in the liturgical renewal.

It is principally by the issuing of directories for pastoral liturgical practice that the authority and zeal of the bishops for the liturgy has been proved. In Italy, there is Cardinal Lecaro's directory for the Mass and the pastoral letter by Cardinal Montini (now Pope Paul VI) on liturgical education (Lent, 1958). In Belgium can be mentioned the directory issued by the bishop of Tournai and those issued by other Belgian bishops. Finally, in France, after the directory authorized by the bishop of Nancy, came that issued on the authority of all the bishops of France. The directory for the Mass (1955) followed that for the sacraments (1951).

The directory for the Mass which appeared to some as a check on their activities proved for the majority of the parochial clergy a decided stimulus; it is a clear manifestation of the rôle of the bishops of France in the liturgical movement, and especially of the national commission, under the chairmanship of the archbishop of Rouen in the name of the Assembly of cardinals and archbishops.

This Assembly, on the other hand, has shown its effective interest in the liturgy by publishing a note on liturgical efforts which unfortunately has not been sufficiently appreciated or utilized.

In any case, it seems quite obvious that the liturgical renewal can only make real progress at the diocesan level. Nothing worthwhile or enduring can be done if the leader of the diocese is not effectively behind it. On the other hand, there is room for considerable hope if the bishop gives sympathetic encouragement to his parish priests. For the bishops are the guardians of the liturgical laws; they have now considerable powers in the matter of liturgical customs and adaptation under the Constitution on worship of the Second Vatican Council.

In these circumstances, the fact that the Second Vatican Council will regulate the position and prerogatives of the bishop in the Church—questions which unfortunately were not reached by the First Vatican Council in 1870—by delineating clearly the active rôle of the bishops in the Church and the steps that they can legitimately take. It may well be thought that this question could with advantage be considered in regard both to the bishops in dechristianized lands and those in missionary territories in the light of the powers recognized by tradition as belonging to the apostolic patriarchs of the East.

Meanwhile, the following example of the action of a liturgical and missionary-minded bishop, working within the Italian liturgical movement, is of interest: we refer to the reforms instituted by Cardinal Lercaro, archbishop of Bologna.

Mgr Moglia was a pioneer of the Italian liturgical renewal; in 1922 he founded at Genoa the *Collegium Tarsicii et Caeciliae* for the liturgical training of the laity; he also founded at Genoa a form of liturgical apostolate with the purpose of joining priests and the younger laity in one and the same liturgical effort. In Mgr Moglia's school were trained the two leaders of the Italian liturgical movement, Cardinal Siri, future archbishop of Genoa, and Cardinal Lercaro, future archbishop of Bologna.

Cardinal Lercaro's liturgical reforms can be grouped together under three heads, each expressive of pastoral concern:

1. *The active participation of the Christian people in the Eucharistic Mystery* which is given concrete form in his directory for the Mass, a practical and complete handbook to enable

the faithful to rediscover the Mass. It encountered great success in Italy and numerous translations were made.

2. *The Paschal Mystery, the centre of all liturgical life*. The
importance of the Paschal Mystery has been emphasized by
the establishment of Lenten "stations", by the children's procession on Palm Sunday and finally by the Mass on Maundy
Thursday which gathers round their bishop all the deans of the
diocese, taking their part on this day as priests, deacons and
subdeacons and expressing, thus, by this *communicatio in
sacris*, the fundamental unity of the liturgical assembly with its
twofold hierarchical and community nature. At the end of this
Mass the deans take the holy oils to their deaneries for distribution to the parish priests. (For the ritual for the reception
of the holy oils in the parishes, see Cardinal Lercaro's *Guida
del Commentatore dei Riti della Settimana Santa*, Bologna,
1959.)

3. *Liturgical training of the faithful* is ensured by a diocesan
centre of liturgical action of which Cardinal Lercaro is president. There are three sections; scientific studies, sacred music
and missionary work are the subjects of conferences given to
the priests of the diocese, thus training a new generation of
clergy who in their turn will ensure the spread of this renewal
of pastoral liturgy in the parishes. In each deanery a priest,
after following a complete course of studies at the centre last-
ing two years, is put in charge of liturgical activities. A centre
for church architecture, also founded by Cardinal Lercaro, in
1955 organized a first congress of architecture and sacred art;
it also publishes a quarterly review, *Chiesa e Quartiere*.

PART II

FUNDAMENTAL IDEAS OF THE LITURGICAL REVIVAL

CHAPTER IV

BIBLE AND LITURGY

LITURGY AND ECUMENISM

The impact of the liturgical revival is not nowadays confined
to the Catholic Church. Similar preoccupations are to be found
elsewhere as well. This corresponds with a general need of
man in our times, and also with new possibilities, arising from
a better knowledge of history and therefore of the original
meaning of rites and attitudes. It is probably necessary to take
this further still; in the psychological context of the world today
it is easier than in preceding centuries to rediscover the real
significance of community and communion.

This state of mind, which forms the foundation of the
ecumenical movement, leads us to emphasize here the ecumenical significance of the liturgical renewal.

The liturgical activity that is going on within the Protestant
Churches[1], and which is well represented by the reformed community at Taizé (Saone-et-Loire), is especially significant in this
respect. The places of worship in certain Protestant Churches
had finally come to look more like lecture halls than places of
worship. The pulpit took the place of the altar, and the neglect
of communion, which formed such a disastrous feature in the
evolution of religious practice among Catholics in the Jan-

---

[1] The problem of the liturgical renewal does not occur in quite the
same way in the Eastern Churches—see Chapter X, p. 121, for what is
said about the Catholic portions of these Churches. The distinction
raised here concerning the Protestant Churches explains why we have
referred to ecumenism at the beginning of this chapter on the Bible;
in the Churches issuing from the Reformation Scripture is given a
privileged and on occasion an exclusive place.

senist centuries, was even more prevalent in the current practice
of Protestantism. The publication, in 1955, by the French Reformed Church, of an "official order of worship" can be
regarded as a turning-point in this history. From the outset, in
the introductory note, care was taken to point out that "this
liturgy takes into account the movement that in our Churches
increases the frequentation and the frequency of the Lord's
Supper. By dissociating it from Sunday worship our Church
was separating itself from the primitive Church." We have
there on one particular point, though it is one of fundamental
importance, evidence of a new spirit which is to be found on
every page of this liturgy which is characterized by the Preface
as follows: "The liturgy, work in common, making its own
Christian prayer of all times and places, is the living and
unanimous prayer of the Church."

This effort is tending to diminish to some extent the diverg-
ence to be found in the past between Protestant worship and
the liturgies of the Latin and the Oriental Churches. This
ecumenical spirit finds expression throughout the Sunday
worship, particularly in the very centre of the celebration of
the Lord's Supper where, after the words of institution, is to
be found the prayer from the Didache: "As the ears of wheat,
once scattered over the mountains, and as the grapes,
once scattered over the hills, are now made one in this bread
and this wine on this table, so Lord, may your Church be
gathered together from the ends of the earth in your kingdom."
The Sunday worship of the new liturgy of the Reformed
Church of France includes also a special mention of the Roman
Church: "We pray you for the Roman Church. Fulfil your
work in her. In our difficult dialogue with her grant us always
to profess the truth in charity."

The example of the Reformed Church of France is of
particular significance. Other Churches which sprang from the
Reformation had preserved greater fidelity to traditional
Western liturgical forms. In England the Oxford Movement
resulted among Anglicans in a certain pastoral and liturgical
renewal; the ritualist movement is one expression of these pre-

occupations. Its influence was to make itself felt on the Continent and particularly in the Church of Sweden where a certain satisfaction began to be felt that the Reformation and adherence to the doctrines of Luther had not totally abolished the traditional liturgy; people usually speak not of a service in a meeting place but indeed of Mass (*mässa*) in a church and the minister of worship is called indifferently "pastor" or "priest" (*präst*). The order of ceremonies in the language of the country follows the order of the Latin liturgy. The liturgical movement, in England as in Sweden, has made a considerable contribution in the preparation of men's minds in both countries for the rôle of capital importance that they have played in the origins of the ecumenical movement. In the same spiritual context a "High Church" movement has also emerged among German Lutherans, as well as among those of Scandinavia.

Simultaneously with this evolution among Protestants, Catholics under the influence of the liturgical renewal were returning to the Bible. Of course, even if there had been no Reformation, the invention of printing would have resulted, sooner or later, in provoking a revival of interest in the Scriptures. Even in those centuries when the masses were illiterate, all the great movements of spiritual renewal in the Church have always included a rediscovery of the Bible. It will be sufficient to recall here St Jerome and the evangelism of St Francis of Assisi.

The division in Western Christendom in the sixteenth century provoked among Catholics reactions of defence and opposition which had held back a movement capable nowadays of reaching maturity more easily, as a result precisely of the need to rediscover, instead of a purely literal fidelity to rites that are somewhat fossilized, the primary inspiration which gave them birth: the whole purpose of the reform instituted by the Second Vatican Council is the return to this primary inspiration.

Catholics and Protestants are able nowadays to appear far less irrevocably opposed to each other than in past centuries. It may well be thought that the day will come when Catholics will no longer consider that they can "fulfil their obligation" by arriving at Mass for the offertory, with little or no interest in the "liturgy of the Word" while Protestants are becoming increasingly aware of the importance of the eucharistic liturgy. The need has been clearly seen for a more complete use of the biblical texts in the liturgy and the reformed Roman Missal, called for by the Second Vatican Council, will contain a more complete course of Scripture readings in place of the previous annual and somewhat arbitrary choice of the same recurring pericopes.

The same need has caused the Church of Sweden to carry out a liturgical reform which, while retaining the lessons of the Roman Missal in the course of a year, regarded as a basic year, proposes other lessons for a second and third year in a way that restores, perhaps not exactly the *lectio continua* of the Fathers, but at least a far more comprehensive meditation of the Scriptures. In the same spirit, there remains to be restored, it would appear, the lessons of the Old Testament which are still almost systematically neglected. In any case, even with the resolution of these questions, it requires to be observed that the hopes raised by the ecumenical movement cannot be better served than by the quest for authenticity and truth in the liturgy.

BIBLE AND LITURGY: THE PRINCIPLES

Whatever the importance of the services rendered by the progress of historical research to the liturgical movement, the liturgical renewal will be neither a return to the Middle Ages, as Dom Guéranger seems to have hoped at the time of the Romantic movement, nor even a return to the age of the Fathers, as Dom Casel seemed to propose; principally it is a return to sources, to the Bible which remains the sacred foundation of all Christian liturgy.

There is a very close connection between the renewal of biblical piety and the liturgical renewal. At the Assisi Congress Cardinal Bea pointed out that "the congregation of the faithful which gathers together for the celebration of the eucharistic sacrifice is the most auspicious place for the reading and fruit-

ful explanation of the Word of God". Indeed it is only in the
context of the liturgy that the Bible is within the comprehension of the great majority of the faithful. Thus it is very necessary for the liturgy to be made apt for this rôle which has too
often been lost sight of in the last centuries.

Just as there is continuity between the Old and the New
Testaments in the unity of the same sacred book, which is the
Bible, so is there continuity between the worship of the Old
Covenant and that of the New, as the Epistle to the Hebrews
puts it. The rite of the paschal lamb prefigures Christ's sacrifice and through it the eucharistic rite of the Christian liturgies.
The synagogal meetings are continued in the Christian liturgy
of the Word: it is significant that the word "synagogue" and the
word "church" are the Greek translation of the same Hebrew
term. The Mass is nothing else than the juxtaposition of these
two liturgies, namely, the liturgy of the word and the eucharistic liturgy.[2]

To speak merely of juxtaposition is an understatement. It is
not only for reasons of convenience that the two liturgies follow
one another immediately. In the fervent Christian communities
at an early date the need was felt for a second meeting for
prayer on Sunday evenings; and this was the origin of the
widespread custom of Vespers. Thus the liturgy of the Word,
it would seem, might well have been separated in this way from
the eucharistic liturgy. Yet since Christian antiquity there is no
trace of such a practice. Right from the time that the first
Christians, excluded from Judaism, no longer frequented the
synagogue, it seems that their worship was immediately
organized in accordance with the fundamental pattern to be
found in all liturgies; a Mass beginning with the liturgy of the
Word and continuing immediately with the eucharistic liturgy,
this latter being placed, so to say, in the prolongation of the
former, since eucharistic communion was preceded by a com-

___

[2] The fundamental difference between worship in the Old and the
New Testaments is mentioned below; in fact, the change in structure
occurred in the "sacrifice", but the "synagogal" setting for prayer remained the same in Christian worship.

munion of minds in faith in the Word of God, liturgically proclaimed.

Even at the end of the Middle Ages this close connection of
the two liturgies of the Mass had not been forgotten. *The
Imitation of Christ* includes a chapter in which the Bible
and the Eucharist are considered together: there are two
"tables" at which the Christian is to be fed—*Una mensa est
sacri altaris, habens panem sanctum, id est Corpus Christi pre-
tiosum, altera est divinae legis, continens doctrinam sanctam*
(Book IV, 11)—"There is one table of the holy altar with the
sacred Bread, that is, the precious Body of Christ, the other is
the table of divine law, with the sacred teaching."

If, nowadays, the Bible has regained a place of honour, a
greater place perhaps than ever before, in the life of the
Christian, if he feels the need to find his true nourishment in it,
particularly in a world where he is tempted by all sorts of
profane reading, in the ordinary course of events he will be led
to pay particular attention to the liturgy of the Word. And he
will do so because fundamentally it is intended to place him in
communion with the Bible and to proclaim it in the congregation of the faithful in fellowship among themselves in their
awareness of being the Church of God. Obviously this is something quite different from a mere reading carried out in isolation, a form of study that can turn into idle curiosity. In the
liturgy the Word of God resounds in the holy place which is
constituted by the gathering together of the members of the
Body of Christ, in the unanimity of a same prayer offered to
the Father in the name of Christ. The proclamation of the
Word is a sacred action, a "sacrament", and it is with the
utmost reverence, in a spirit of adoration, that it is to be
received.

In these conditions, preaching no longer appears as an inter-
lude or something extra. It forms an integral part of the
liturgical action. There can be no question of giving a lesson,
or a conference, of making a show of oratory or wit; rather
must the preacher, in the name of the bishop, the successor of
the apostles, open the minds of his hearers to the understand-

ing of the Word of God. For the sermon is a part of the liturgical celebration: the celebrant officiates, *locum tenens*, taking the place of Christ himself, both when he preaches and when he pronounces the words of consecration. All that the congregation hears, whether it is the sacred readings or the homily, although of course in different degrees and varying intensity, is received by it as a living Word, always a reality because it is a message of an eternal nature, addressed to it by Christ himself, present in its midst.

BIBLE AND LITURGY: THE FACTS

It must be admitted that the foregoing ideas have been quite lost from view during the past few centuries. It has even been said that if the Protestant is a Christian for whom after the sermon is over the rest is of little account, the Catholic is one who does not mind arriving at Mass for the offertory and makes a point of missing the sermon. There is a germ of truth in this caricature. The popularization of a certain form of casuistry led to the belief that the liturgy of the Word was unimportant and to some extent optional; arrival at Mass before the end of the *Credo* "fulfilled the obligation". Thus the Word is proclaimed before the congregation has gathered together, in a half-empty church, amid the noise of people arriving.

This is an entire reversal of the whole aspect of the congregation gathered for the liturgy in comparison with what it was formerly. In earlier days it was the liturgy of the Word which was the most crowded since the catechumens and penitents left at the beginning of the eucharistic liturgy in which they did not take part. At the present time, many of those present at the eucharistic liturgy come to it to fulfil a precept of the Church whose real meaning they do not even seek to understand. And there have even been occasions in the past when there has been refusal to give communion during Mass, just as it was sometimes urged that it was better to communicate before Mass in order to be able to make a proper thanksgiving, if there was no time for it after Mass. This shows clearly that

the whole meaning of eucharistic liturgy had been lost sight of,
for Eucharist, as the term shows (but it is a Greek word), is
nothing else than a thanksgiving.

It is, of course, easy to discover a certain number of factors
that contributed to this lack of understanding of the Mass. The
meaning of the Bible, which is quite naturally made clear
where proclamation of the Word does not take place, para-
doxically, in a language that has become incomprehensible to
the congregation, had become foreign to the faithful. And this
despite the care taken to read the translation of the Gospel
before the sermon. Moreover, the latter has not always been
preached on the texts of the day's liturgy. The almost complete freedom left to the preacher, in sharp contrast with the
inflexibility of the rubrics, enabled him to consider other
passages with no concern for those just read, and thus to com-
pensate in some measure for the disadvantages arising from the
fact that year by year the same passages from the Bible were
read on the same days, while the remainder of the sacred text
was never officially proclaimed to the people.

What is astonishing in all this is not the uneasiness increasingly felt in the face of such a situation, but that it could have
come about and endured for so long without anything being
done about it until the end of 1963 with the promulgation of
the decree of the Second Vatican Council. It would be outside
the scope of this book to discuss the historical reasons for such
a state of affairs in order to understand a point of view that is
undoubtedly outmoded nowadays. It will be sufficient to note
the fact of a returning awareness of traditional values that were
lost to view for too long.

CONCLUSION

"Word of God and word of man, all proclaim the Mystery
and thus, in the liturgical structure of the Mass, we pass
naturally from the proclamation of the Word of God to the
sacramental celebration: there is no word without sacrament,
no sacrament without liturgy of the Word. We have access to

the Mystery only through the theology of the Word of God, which is Christ, the intervention of God in history, the recapitulation, the new beginning and the definitive condition of history." As was thus well said at the Strasbourg congress in 1957, without understanding of the Bible the liturgy remains only an illegible sign. That is why the catechumens, in ancient times, before having access to the eucharistic Mystery had for long been made familiar with the Bible through the liturgy of the Word in which they took part from the time of their admission to the catechumenate.

APPENDIX: THE PROBLEM OF THE MISSAL

As was pointed out above, the honour of first popularizing the translation of the Missal with explanatory notes for the use of the faithful in modern times must be attributed to Dom Gérard van Caloen and Dom Gaspar Lefebvre. Nowadays, Missals for the use of the laity exist in so many editions and formats that it is difficult even to offer a list of them. It will be useful however to mention here certain matters of more general interest in this connection.

Properly speaking the Missal is no affair of the congregation's. The lessons are read aloud in order to be heard and not to be read by each one in private. The anthems (introit, offertory, communion) are the refrains of processional chants meant to be sung and not read rapidly.

In fact, in the present state of affairs, and even with the people's part of the Mass in the vernacular, the Missal has a part to play in the liturgy, and it has certainly made a contribution to the liturgical revival. Dom Lefebvre's Missal, for example, has done much to educate the more fervent among the faithful. It can also be said that the Missal is and will always remain a valid means of personal liturgical study. In particular, the Missal helps the faithful to grasp the fundamental connection between the Bible and the liturgy. Everything, or almost everything in the Missal, is either taken directly from the Bible or at least directly inspired by biblical texts. It might even be said that the Missal is the Bible re-composed by the Church for the purpose of the liturgical year. Moreover, good editions of the Missal always give the scriptural references. Thus the principal events of the history of salvation are re-lived through the liturgical cycle and the Missal thereby becomes a very living and spiritual introduction to the Bible.

These advantages of a Missal, however, must not cause us to lose sight of the fact that in the first place liturgical celebration is *hierarchical*. There should be no question of everyone reading silently whatever the celebrant, reader or choir read or sing. Each individual should play his proper part in the celebration. Then, the Mass is a *community affair*; it is not a silent gathering of individuals with their noses in their books. The church on Sunday is not a reading room or, to quote a comparison made by Cardinal Lercaro, a restaurant where each person appears to be taking his meal in isolation. The emphasis placed by the Second Vatican Council on the congregation's participation should go far to make such an individualist approach impossible.

CHAPTER V

LITURGY AND CATECHESIS

"Catechesis" is a fashionable word at the present time. Its facile use in reviews and conferences may well deprive it in a short time of any precise meaning. It can be recalled simply that the term "catechesis" implies the presentation of the Christian message in a fairly developed and elaborated form. Thus catechesis is to be distinguished from kerygmatic proclamation which simply announces the message of Christ, who died and rose again for us, with no attempt to elaborate its implications.

But the patristic flavour of the word catechesis immediately conjures up the biblical, liturgical and spiritual context, together with implications of conversion and initiation which the less high-sounding term of "religious instruction" seems to exclude. Nevertheless, religious instruction, if it is true to its name, implies everything included in catechesis, and it must be admitted, if for the moment we forget the fleeting magic of words, that at the present time religious instruction and catechesis are synonyms.

And so there will be several forms of catechesis—of children at the age of reason, of adolescents, of catechumens, of adults. In some cases the emphasis will be on initiation, in others more importance will be given to bringing out the religious understanding of the message and its coherence. But in all cases it is the same duty of education of faith that is being discharged.

So far as the subject of the present chapter is concerned it must be pointed out that a considerable effort is required in pastoral liturgy to make clear the need for liturgical life by means of teaching. This liturgical catechesis, following the example of the Roman Catechism of the Council of Trent and of the Ritual, is principally conceived as preaching on the sacraments based on the rites themselves in accordance with the method used by the Fathers of the Church.

LITURGY AN ILLEGIBLE SIGN WITHOUT CATECHESIS

It is an absolute necessity for those in a human world, in a world of signs, and not only of things, that they should be initiated into the meaning of these signs. Without this knowledge they will be lost, just as they would be in a foreign country of whose language and customs they were ignorant. Those who "know" have to impart knowledge of these signs, gestures and customs of the community to those who come from outside and "do not know". Especially must initiates reveal to those who are not the ends pursued by the community and how the signs, gestures and customs used serve the ideal which gathers the community together.

Therefore catechesis is needed for the uninitiated, for the catechumens and for those whose position is tantamount to being a catechumen. But catechesis is necessary also for the initiates, even for the most fervent, so that continually they can revitalize their liturgical observance by thorough study and by ceaselessly returning to fundamentals; otherwise, it is more than likely that they will fall into formalism and entire lack of understanding.

Both for initiates, and for others as well, the mental effort required for understanding of the liturgy is no small one. The liturgical Constitution of the Second Vatican Council has indeed laid down that the rites "should be distinguished by a noble simplicity" and that they should be "short, clear and unencumbered by any useless repetitions"; they are to be "within the people's powers of comprehension" and not require normally very much explanation. Yet it still remains true that the whole universe of worship is difficult for modern man, the product of a civilization very different from that in which the Church's worship grew up; even with a reformed liturgy catechesis will be necessary, though possibly to a smaller degree than hitherto. Its purpose, therefore, is to decipher for us the whole universe which has grown up outside us, and to communicate to us the minimum that is indispensable to enable us to be at ease in our own fatherland.

THIS CATECHESIS WILL BE BIBLICAL

Thus, just like the biblical renewal, the liturgical renewal implies a certain cultural concern. And there is nothing astonishing in the fact that the concern for liturgical culture is to be found in those countries where the general cultural movement is most active. It is the duty of the clergy to watch over and satisfy this need of culture among Christian people. Good intentions and pastoral zeal are insufficient to bring this culture into play. Both pastors and people must be willing to make the effort to enter a foreign land and receive the biblical texts used in the liturgy. In some sort, it means entering a land that is doubly foreign, for liturgical tradition has transplanted biblical texts into a very different cultural context from that in which they first saw light of day. Pastors, if they wish to educate their people, must be in a position to obtain some grasp of the relativism of the different cultures that biblical and liturgical tradition has passed through during the centuries. In the endeavour to acquire this liturgical culture some idea of historical relativity must be shown, a quality which only too often is lacking and yet is one which enables what is essential, enduring and of present importance to be sifted out from the various cultural forms that the Bible and the liturgy have assumed. The danger nowadays is one of superficiality, of pastors being satisfied with "timeless" commentaries through lack of knowledge of the vital situations in which the liturgical forms arose, developed or, on the contrary, became fossilized.

But the other danger is to remain at the stage of mere

historical explanation without spiritual implications for the faithful; lack of theology is the cause of this. A certain type of liturgical exegesis, inadequate in all speculative thought, which does not seek to reach what is permanent, and therefore of real interest, is impoverishing for pastor and faithful alike for it takes no count of the essential, personal and community needs of our religious life.

What we need is an authentic understanding of the rites without our getting bogged down in the necessary but inadequate archeological investigation. It requires to be repeated that, for the lack of speculative effort, of an all-embracing and unifying viewpoint, the liturgical movement is in danger of seeing its pastoral influence diminish. But this effort of thought must always be exerted on the basis of the rites themselves. Thought about the liturgy is no initiation to the liturgy, it is the liturgy which initiates to the liturgy—on condition that its catechesis is enlightened, properly elaborated and communicated. For the liturgy itself is a catechesis and it is this which we have now to examine.

THE LITURGY IS ITSELF CATECHESIS

The liturgy is itself catechesis. It is intended to "guide the faithful to a conscious Christianity". The liturgy is catechesis by reason of the Word of God which it transmits. This immediately raises the problem of the hearing and understanding of the Word of God by the people. The subject is treated below in connection with the subject of liturgical language.

As the vehicle of the Word of God the liturgy forms the normal introduction to the Bible and it is by means of the passages proclaimed in the liturgical assembly that people are normally to be led to a taste for and an understanding of the Scriptures. But the matter must be regarded in realist fashion and it must be recognized that this introduction to the Bible by means of the liturgy is effected only very partially by reason of the present form of the liturgy. A selection of short passages, often arbitrarily chosen, can hardly constitute a genuine introduction to the Bible. What is required is a restoration of the *lectio continua*, that is, the consecutive, well ordered systematic presentation of the principal biblical passages suitably adapted to a given community. The present system of lessons, represented by the Sunday Epistles and Gospels, is only haphazard and therefore unable to provide a catechesis worthy of the name, that is, of communicating a spirit and a form of thought. A better selection of passages of Scripture is promised in the reformed Roman Missal to be issued in due course.

What is the place of the sermon is this catechetical dimension of the liturgy? It has to be recognized that considerable progress has been made in the course of half a century. In 1913 the French Jesuit review *Études* began a controversy— one that is nowadays quite an affair of the past—by publishing an article by Fr Navatel, S.J., on "The Liturgical Apostolate and Personal Piety". In it the liturgy was defined as the perceptible ceremonial and ornamental part of Catholic worship, contrasting with it, among other things, preaching.

It is generally recognized nowadays that the sermon is a liturgical act. And this has been made quite clear by the Constitution on Liturgy passed by the Second Vatican Council. Preaching does not form a sort of parenthesis in the Mass. It must be regarded in such a way that it can be integrated into the liturgy. The sermon has its starting point in the celebration and leads to a more enlightened and united celebration. That is its nature. The Sunday sermon is not in the same category as a Lenten course which is intended to give systematic and exhaustive teaching on a particular subject, or a mission sermon which should cause its audience to discover afresh the heavy and exacting requirements of Christian life. That is why it is more normal for the celebrant himself, and not some priest in a surplice who happens to be on duty that day, to give the Sunday sermon.

Again, liturgy is catechesis through its rites, and through the gestures and attitudes that it requires of the community.

These rites, gestures and attitudes convey a spirit, they direct the development of the religious mentality in individuals and communities. They are the primary form, anterior to words, of the total Christian mentality. Thus the liturgy is a catechesis which embraces the whole being. Through liturgical observance doctrinal values are in some sort verified because they are apprehended in an experience. The liturgy is the royal road maintaining a close link between doctrine and life.

It must even be said that the liturgy leads to a moral commitment. It places us in an attitude of listening, offering and obedience in relation to God, of fellowship in relation to our brothers. It disposes us to act in a Christian way, and this without moralism. But that does not mean that the liturgy is in a position automatically to educate Christian behaviour in all its practical decisions. Ivan the Terrible seemed to take part in the liturgy of his times with his whole soul while giving evidence in his behaviour of a state of mind at utter variance with Christianity. At the other end of the scale, there is an approach to morality, as for example in the post-Tridentine school of casuistry, which is entirely unconnected with liturgy.

The Christian education effected by the liturgy is something at a far deeper level than any particular approach to the subject. The liturgy imbues us with the fundamental themes of the faith by making us live in that relationship which it establishes between God and us. In the liturgy, indeed, we do not pray in a sentimental fashion or in a state of spiritual independence, but by relying on the truths of faith. The eucharistic prefaces are rich in doctrinal themes: they are the creeds—the symbols of the faith—in action. And in its festive aspect the liturgy sets before us doctrinal truths in the most suitable way to motivate Christian joy (Jungmann, *MD* 47-8, pp. 55-6).

Year by year the liturgy educates us to a further deepening of our understanding of the fundamental Christian truths and values, to thanksgiving and to our approach to God through Christ (*per Christum Dominum nostrum*). Every year it causes us to celebrate the redemptive mysteries (events) of our Lord. "When thus week by week, year by year, our Lord and his work appear to the spiritual gaze of the faithful, they must come to understand very well what it means to be a Christian."

That is why Christianity has been able to continue to exist at periods when there was no preaching, when there was no reading. That is why it continues still to exist in vast regions like Russia where the liturgical celebrations are the only means of religious activity. There is no Christian truth that is not expressed in one way or another by the liturgy. In Pius XI's phrase, "the liturgy is the principal organ of the ordinary magisterium of the Church".

Liturgical education, following the example of the cate-chumenate in patristic times, must form part of the first intro-duction to the faith. A great step forward was taken when it was rediscovered that already in adherence and awakening to the faith the part to be played by the rites of the Church was of capital importance. In practice in many places converts (that is, catechumens) are interviewed individually in an office or room attached to the church for the purpose of receiving a series of instructions from a priest or a nun. And it is to these in-dividual interviews that the catechumen's contact with the Church is confined until the day of his baptism. But since 1962 there has been the possibility for the catechumen while following the course of instruction for baptism to take part in community rites by means of which the faith that he comes to ask of the Church is not only explained but made active. It was in 1962, in fact, that the Congregation of Rites gave permission for the rite for the baptism of adults to be per-formed in seven distinct steps, spaced out in accordance with the progress made in catechetical instruction. This permission has been confirmed and enlarged in the Constitution on liturgy of the Second Vatican Council. It lays down that the cate-chumenate for adults is to be restored and to comprise several distinct stages. "In this way, the time of the catechumenate, which is intended to be a period of suitable instruction, may be sanctified by sacred rites" which are to be celebrated at definite intervals during the period of preparation for baptism.

THE PROBLEM OF LITURGICAL LANGUAGE

It would be wrong to think that the liturgical Constitution of the Second Vatican Council has finally abolished Latin as the liturgical language of the Roman rite. On the contrary it states quite clearly that the "use of the Latin language is to be preserved in the Latin rites". On the other hand, it has made wide concessions for the use of the mother tongue in the public worship of the Church, in the Mass, the administration of the sacraments and other parts of the liturgy, so that *in practice*, with the permission of the local hierarchies, what amounts to the people's part of the liturgy may be in the vernacular, together with much else besides.

The debate that has gone on ever since Trent over the use of the mother tongue in the worship of the Roman rite is in its own way another manifestation of the left-right or conservative-progressive conflict. And the controversy over liturgical language has also been in part a cultural conflict. This cultural aspect of the problem of Latin and its historical origins has been analysed by Cyril Korolevsky:

> In the sixteenth century the doctrinal errors of Protestants led to a strong reaction at the Council of Trent. But the Council nevertheless did not formally condemn the principle of the use of living languages in public worship, considered in itself; what it did was to forbid such use on the ground that it was inopportune at that time, and because of the very great prestige which Latin still enjoyed. However, the circumstances of this prohibition were not properly understood, and it brought about a state of mind in which an opportune measure of suitability was interpreted as a formal condemnation; and this mentality governed all that was done during the succeeding centuries.
>
> Today, the increasing desire of many clergy and people for "more vernacular", the development of the liturgical movement, pastoral requirements and the need to make public worship more intelligible if Christianity is to continue to hold people in contemporary conditions, have led to experiments some of which are not happy; and this increases the desire and need for a reform. . . .

Quite involuntarily, the community of faithful is split between two categories: those, generally the economically better off, who have some classical culture and can understand and appreciate the Roman liturgy, and those who do not understand it properly and have no means of doing so. The Church is the society of all the faithful; but if there be, to use the modern jargon, a sort of bourgeois aristocracy among them, then the exclusive use of Latin at public worship tends not to unify but to divide.[1]

Fr A. M. Roguet wrote as follows:

The whole of Mass proclaims the Word of God. If the Word is not understood, it is not a word. And if it is understood only by means of a Missal and individual effort it is no longer the Word of God in public worship which is understood by me. I receive the Word of God, of course, but through the inter-mediary of an instrument lacking authority and in the solitude and uncertainty of my own personal study.... And so it is to be hoped that one day the Holy See will put into effect the resolution that it has itself approved (at the Lugano Congress): that the celebrant may one day proclaim the Word of God directly in the language of the faithful.[2]

The people must understand the liturgy and the liturgy must increase the understanding of the faith by the people. For this to come about the liturgical language must be within the grasp of the faithful. And indeed such was the practice of the Church. The primitive Church, as she made her way into the Greek world, at once adopted the Greek language instead of clinging to Aramaic. When she spread from the Greek com-munities to take root among the peoples of the West she adopted Latin to make herself understood.

We should not be surprised that the expression "Latin, the language of the Church" is entirely incomprehensible and in-deed unthinkable with reference to a Christian of the East, even a Catholic, if it denotes a certain exclusivism. Latin is a language of the Church, it is even the language for a

[1] Cyril Korolevsky, *Living Languages in Catholic Worship* (London and Westminster, Md, 1957), pp. 113–14, 164.
[2] *Parole de Dieu et liturgie*, IV, p. 140.

privileged period of a Church which is the Mother of all the Churches of the West and moderator of all the others, and to this extent Latin belongs to the universal Church, as a common possession, but no more.

Moreover, it must be recognized, as Canon Martimort has pointed out, "that the discipline of the Western Church on the subject of liturgical language is far from being as severe as it appears at first sight; it is even capable of evolving according to circumstances and might well, one day, from missionary necessity come to match the practice of the Greek and Egyptian missionaries."[3]

The three authors quoted above were writing, of course, before the Second Vatican Council, but in dealing with the history and development of the liturgical movement it was necessary to show how the climate of opinion has changed in the course of the last quarter of a century. Twenty-five years ago, although the possibility of an extensive use of the vernacular was being canvassed in some quarters, generally speaking it was held that such a change of practice would be against the "mind of the Church", though the exact meaning of this last expression was never very clearly defined. Then came the Second World War. That and its aftermath brought home very sharply to many working among prisoners of war, with the armed forces or in the great industrial centres, the need for a living liturgy and the impossibility of any serious progress so long as worship, that is, the *public* worship of the Church, was conducted in a dead language. This is the explanation of the change, a change that appears to many as a complete revolution, that has been enacted by the Second Vatican Council.

In the Constitution on liturgy there are references to an extended use of the vernacular in the rites of the Church. Although Latin remains the language of the Roman rite it is conceded that the "use of the mother tongue is frequently of great advantage to the people in the Mass, the administration of the sacraments and in other parts of the liturgy". This con-

[3] *MD* 11, 84, 130.

cession is to apply in the first place to the lessons (Epistle and Gospels, etc.) at Mass and to those prayers and chants which are the congregation's part in the rite. In addition the whole of the rites for the administration of the sacraments may be in the mother tongue and this includes even the essential forms. At the same time the Council has called for a large measure of revision in the Roman Ritual because, as it pointed out in the Constitution, with the passage of time "there have crept into the rites of the sacraments and sacramentals certain features which have rendered their nature and purpose far from clear to the people of today so that changes are necessary to adapt them to the needs of our times".

Thus it is clear that what is here implied is a far larger question than the understanding of a language. It must not be imagined that when the Word of God and the liturgical texts have been translated they will automatically become intelligible. Think, for example, of the difficulty encountered by an average congregation in taking part in the Easter vigil, even when preparation has been made for it by instruction on the various symbols of fire, water, light and so on. What is needed is a whole education of the congregation in their entire approach to the Easter mystery; this cannot be reduced to a question of Latin or English. Continuous effort over the whole field is required to raise the faithful to the level of liturgical understanding. In this way, by providing Christian people with suitable instruction, will be laid the foundations of a liturgy more adapted to its purpose, for then both people and hierarchy will realize the appropriate conditions for a living liturgy.

Lastly, it may be well to return to a point of view mentioned above. The position adopted by the Church with respect to the special problem of liturgical language or languages will depend on the way in which she is able to solve the more general problem of culture in the modern world. Between the nationalist movements, which she must take into account, and her universal vocation, a fundamental attitude is still easy enough to determine. It is more difficult to conceive and create a culture for humanity which without doubt is seeking unity and, on the basis of this culture, liturgical forms in relation with it. This cultural aspect of the problem is brought out clearly by the following quotation from Möhler, the great German theologian, which will serve as a conclusion to this part of the book:

> In all circumstances of life every people makes use of the language which God has given it; why then do we not make the finest use possible of this divine gift, namely in the communication of religious sentiments during the most solemn action of the whole of our worship? Am I not therefore to put before God a prayer of thanksgiving in the language which he has given me? And if the language of the liturgy must itself be changed, with an essential perfection of the national language, is not that in the nature of things? Would we thereby accuse God of not having given each people its perfect language at the outset? Language is always the most perfect image of the cultural state of a people; thus its language, whatever it is, is always the best for it.

The Second Vatican Council, by leaving to the local hierarchies the application of the provisions for the introduction of the vernacular in worship, has recognized the existence of the cultural problem alluded to above and, by implication, the truth of Möhler's remarks in the foregoing quotation.

CHAPTER VI

LITURGY AND CHRISTIAN
LIFE

The starting point and the principal features of the fundamental ideas of the liturgical movement emphasized here are to
be found almost completely in the work of Dom Odo Casel,
monk of Maria Laach. In Chapter VII of his book *Life and
Liturgy*[1] Fr Bouyer has given a well-balanced and critical
explanation of this work and of the doctrine elaborated in it.
We cannot do better than quote Fr Bouyer's explanation of
Dom Casel's teaching on the Christian mystery.

But what, then, is the Christian mystery? If we mean to ask
what it is in its deepest reality, it is nothing less than the *tran-
situs*, the passage from death to life, by faith, through the cross
to the resurrection, which was once for all accomplished in
Christ. The Mystery, therefore, is an action; and it is an action
which took place in the past and can never be repeated, because
it is perfect. The Mystery is the cross of Jesus, the cross seen
primarily as an accomplishment . . . the cross seen also in the
fullness of its wonderful fecundity, that is, as including the resurrection of Christ, his ascension into glory, and, through the
Christ who has now himself become *Pneuma*, life-giving Spirit,
the radiance of all the wonderful gifts which he has given to
man. This action is as it were the inner essence of the Mystery.
But the Mystery is permanently embodied in the liturgy—more
especially in the Mass, but also in all the sacraments and even
in the sacramentals, in the Divine Office, in the feasts of the

[1] American edn, *Liturgical Piety*. See Select Bibliography.

liturgical year, and in the whole Christian life, since this life is
nothing less than the expansion of what is given in the sacramental order. In all this, of course, the mystery is hidden.
Nothing is present of the historical circumstances by which the
divine action was set in its place in time and space. But the substance of the action is present, in a mysterious way, entirely
real to faith; and it is through this substance that the Christ-
Pneuma encounters the lives of all men and diffuses in them
his own life.

The grace of Christ cannot be separated from his Person; his
life *in* us is not a different thing from his life lived *among* us
and for us ... in and through the liturgy, the all-saving act of
Christ, giving life through his death, is truly and really present
in its fullness as in its unity.[2]

In this explanation of Christian worship Dom Casel took as
his starting-point the "mysteries", a term used as a common
name for the Eastern religions which were being introduced
into the Roman Empire at about the same time as Christianity.
Each of them was a *dromenon*, that is, a kind of religious
drama, the liturgical representation of the death and resurrection of a god. By being associated, in the actual performance
of this representation, with the saving act of the deity, the
initiates or "mystes" were to be saved. They were to be thought
of as born again to a new and divine life, the life of the god
himself triumphing over death.

For Dom Casel, these mysteries were a sort of providential
preparation in human nature for what God was to do for it in
Christ. The pagan mysteries did not, properly speaking, influence the beginnings of Christianity, but they provided a frame
for Christianity to fill with its divine grace, the pattern which
would make that grace appealing to human nature, as showing
how grace brought with it precisely what human nature most
desires and had been attempting to attain for itself. Christianity had really given in the liturgical mysteries what pagan-
ism had only contrived to adumbrate or desire in its
"mysteries".

[2] Bouyer, *op. cit.*, pp. 87–8.

There is no difficulty in seeing the importance of this point of view, not only for the history of Christianity but also, and especially, for the spiritual life of the Christian. For this spiritual life can no longer be considered as a quest, and still less as an individual adventure, under the guidance of personal imagination, sentiment, intelligence and will. But all these faculties joined together will find in perfect assimilation to the person of Christ the effective realization of the destiny of the human person, and this assimilation is effected ordinarily by means of the liturgy. The liturgy gives to all those who come to it the mystery of Christ, as a personal destiny which is offered as an integration, a personalization of the destiny of man both as individual and as community.

This economy of the mystery of salvation must indeed form a protection for the destiny of thousands of human beings who do not normally or visibly come into contact with it. Here we have the whole problem of the salvation of the unbeliever. But having raised this important distinction, we do not feel it an exaggeration to state that Dom Casel's theory offers the most realist and most rewarding view of the Christian life.

In fact, it is a doctrine rather than a theory and it has been handed down to us by the Fathers of the Church and liturgical tradition. It has certainly been keenly debated and it must be admitted, with Fr Bouyer especially, that its historical foundation based on the parallel between Christian mystery and pagan mystery does not stand up. But even if these and other corrections are admitted, it may still well be thought that this doctrine of the mystery, far from being contrary to the ordinary teaching of the Church, is in agreement with it on many of its fundamental and catechetical aspects. For a better understanding of the mystery of Christian worship, and for a clear comparison of the teaching of the Encyclical *Mediator* with Dom Casel's ideas, which at one time some chose to see in opposition with each other, we reproduce here a part of the comparison made by Dom Hild between Pius XII's teaching and Dom Casel's thought:

The liturgy is living and transcendent, it is worship, the whole priestly life of Christ and his Church. . . . The eucharistic mystery is the mystery of worship par excellence, it is the liturgy. . . . Holy Mass is shown as being truly a mystery of worship and not as being purely and simply a commemoration of the passion and death of Christ. Sacramentally, Christ is present and does again what he once did for us. . . . The whole Christ . . . in all the states of his existence is present in the liturgical mystery. . . . The liturgical presence of the whole Christ is expressed as the mystery of the Christian feast (Dom Casel's expression, *Festenmysterium*). The liturgical year, in so far as it is something sacred, in so far as it is mystery, must guide and nourish Christian piety.[3]

The Encyclical again tells us clearly that living the liturgical year consists not only in meditation on the mysteries of salvation, but especially in contact with Christ himself. For "the liturgical year . . . is not a cold and lifeless representation of the events of the past, or a simple and bare record of a former age. It is rather Christ himself who is ever living in his Church. Here he continues that journey of immense mercy which he lovingly began in his mortal life . . . with the design of bringing men to know his mysteries and in a way to live by them."

In a very special way these mysteries of Christ are the sacraments. But the Encyclical *Mediator* says more than once that "Christ is present not only in the Mass and the sacraments, but in every liturgical action, and even in the Divine Office in which the Church prays in common with her Lord and Bridegroom. Every liturgical act is an act of Christ himself, every liturgical rite constitutes a *sacramentum*, it contains and effects what it signifies."

It is obvious that this way of putting things necessarily takes us back beyond the scholastic formulas to the Fathers' ampler presentation. Now that is the teaching of the mystery of Christian worship. That does not mean to say, however, that at present it has been completely formulated. Dom Casel's scholarly elaboration of it—somewhat encumbered perhaps by

[3] From an article in *Les Questions liturgiques et paroissiales* 48, 186–203.

its historical setting—still stands in need of a formulation that is, so to say, kerygmatic, and can be incorporated in the people's catechesis and faith, just as the narrower formulation of scholastic theology has been.

Now it is this that the Encyclical *Mediator* means to teach us by asserting so clearly the presence of Christ in every liturgical act. This sacramental realism, in harmony with the mystery of the Church as a whole, is strictly speaking the mystery of worship. And by this mystery our Lord genuinely perpetuates his redemption in the Church, leading us all in his train in an ever increasing eschatological perspective to the Parousia, *donec veniat*.

Dom Casel found in this point of view a perfect expression of his own views, but it remains to be seen whether all the details of his particular teaching on the Christian mystery will stand the test of time. The Second Vatican Council does not refer to the subject like *Mediator*, though in its definition of the liturgy and its remarks on the Christian year it reflects the climate of opinion provoked by Casel's work. Thus it can be seen that it is from the liturgy that in reality Christian life is to be derived, since it is in the liturgy that, through Jesus Christ, we can come to an encounter with the living God. "Under the species of an evocation of the past, the liturgy brings to us in the present Christ in person."

There follows from this—it is a subsidiary point but of great importance—the hope of a Christian revival as a result of the whole liturgical reform initiated under Pius XII with the revision of the Holy week rites and continued by the Second Vatican Council in more radical fashion. The Paschal Mystery, the fundamental mystery of our worship, has been restored to the centre of Christian life. It is not merely a rubrical change, but Christian life which has been restored to its true sources.

In concluding this account of Dom Casel's teaching, and of its confirmation by the magisterium of the Church, it is worth while pointing out that he himself gave no ordinary witness to the value of his theological synthesis through his whole life of prayer and contemplation, and also by his death which occurred just as he had sung the *Lumen Christi* in the Easter Vigil:

> Just as he had saluted with a loud voice the Light of Christ and was about to celebrate the Easter praise (*praeconium paschale*), our well-beloved Father in Christ, the devoted servant of the sacred mystery and initiator into its richness, Odo Casel, monk of Laach, made perfect in his holocaust and, passing over with his Lord during the holy night, entered into the blessed vision, being made perfect by means of the paschal mysteries which he himself had handed on to the initiates. *Deo gratias*!

This mortuary card, by any token, is one of the finest texts of the contemporary liturgical movement.

LITURGY, SPIRITUALITY AND DEVOTIONS

In our treatment of Dom Casel's teaching we quoted Fr Bouyer's account of it. We return to the same source for an introduction to the subject which it seemed appropriate to add at the end of this chapter.

In chapter XVIII of *Life and Liturgy* Fr Bouyer gives the following rough sketch of the evolution of devotions in the Church:

> Formerly the liturgy comprehended the whole prayer-life of the Church and of all Christians; and therefore there was no problem [of the relation between liturgical life and spiritual life]. For the Christians of antiquity, the liturgy was not only a school of prayer, *the* school of prayer, but it *was* their prayer. In the collective prayer each took his own part and so made it his own most personal prayer; thus a prayer which was nourished by that of the whole community brought back to the prayer of the whole community the spiritual fruit which each person had derived.[4]

Fr Bouyer goes on to show how the liturgy began to grow fossilized at the turning point of the Middle Ages and how the people, unable to understand it, took no further interest in

[4] Bouyer, *op. cit.*, p. 243.

it. Then came the Franciscans and Dominicans who provided a vigorous evangelical impulse. They developed a type of piety centred on the humanity of Christ and the human feelings that such an emphasis could provoke. "The cleavage between liturgical and 'popular' piety had begun and could only continue to widen." There even occurred the development of a kind of neoplatonic mysticism which of its nature was completely uninterested in the strongly historical and factual aspect of the liturgical mystery; it was supplemented by the great and beautiful mysticism of the Rhenish school. At the same time, among the Benedictines and Cistercians occurred a decline of liturgical understanding which was exemplified by the accretions to the Office and, especially for the lay brothers, by the multiplication of devotions—Rosary, Way of the Cross and so on. Somewhat later came the "new worship in the Blessed Sacrament of a presence which was visualized more and more as an ordinary human kind of presence, increasingly separated from the Mass and even from communion" which threatened "to wipe out the whole idea of the sacramental order and of the presence of Christ *in mysterio*".

But what are we to do now? We must certainly not abolish at one stroke all forms of popular devotion, but, as *Mediator* and the Second Vatican Council both propose, we should endeavour gently and firmly to bring such practices back to the norm of authentic liturgy, to permeate them with its spirit and finally develop into an auxiliary of the liturgy what originated as a substitute for it. This indeed clearly seems to be the mind of the Council when it lays down that the popular devotions of Christian people are to be highly commended "provided that they are in agreement with the laws and norms of the Church, above all when they are ordered by the Holy See". Devotions proper to local churches, we are told, have a special dignity if they are "undertaken by mandate of the bishops according to customs or books lawfully approved", but they are to be so composed that they are "in harmony with the liturgical seasons in the sacred liturgy"; in addition they must in some sense be derived from the latter and so "lead the people to it", since of its very nature "the liturgy far surpasses any of them".

The devotional practice which above all others can be regenerated in the light of the liturgy is certainly the Rosary. But this is also the case with the more modern devotion to the Sacred Heart, without mentioning the Month of Mary of which Fr de Féligonde said, "But it is purely and simply Advent". Considerations such as these bring us

> finally to the truth which will give an organic unity to all our observations concerning ways in which devotions may be brought once more into the current of the liturgy rather than be cast aside by it. The fundamental approach to the problem of uniting personal, psychological and therefore subjective devotion with the objective discovery of the Mystery in the liturgical tradition must always be that of restoring that Christian culture apart from which liturgy must always fossilize and so become incapable of transmitting the life of which it is so full. This means that the first and fundamental condition for any liturgical revival which is truly a revival of piety must be a personal knowledge of the whole Bible and meditation on it, both to be achieved along the lines laid out for us by the liturgy; such a revival implies a full acceptance of the Bible as Word of God and as the framework and everliving source of authentic Christianity.[5]

As a conclusion to this section on liturgy, spirituality and devotions we set down here three principles:

1. The perspective revealed by this pastoral liturgical approach appears as the most comprehensive of all. Far from rejecting forms of spirituality and devotions which tended to supplant the liturgy, on the contrary it takes possession of them.

2. What makes the unity between liturgical and non-liturgical spirituality and devotion is on a last analysis the Word of God. It is in the Bible that the community celebration and personal prayer nourish each other, both feeding on this same Word of God. In these conditions, forms of spiritu-

[5] Bouyer, *op. cit.*, p. 253.

ality, devotion and various practices can be considered as special approbations of revelation, liturgy itself being the universal approbation (because belonging to the Mystery) for all Christians gathered together in the unity of the faith. *Mysterium fidei.*

3. But when this has been done, and agreement easily reached on these points, it seems to us that the essential still remains to be said. In fact the problem raised by this real conflict between liturgy, spirituality and devotions goes beyond the setting usually assigned to it. In fact, it is the whole problem of Christian existence which is thus raised, in all its dimensions of the sacred set within a profane world. For after all, what is it that makes a Christian to be a Christian? Is it the liturgy? Is it the practice of some devotion or other? Is it authentic incorporation in a certain school of spirituality or some branch of Catholic Action?

In all the possible answers to these questions, what are we to think of the place given to the sick, the poor, children? Which is the most meritorious on Easter night, to sing in choir at the vigil service or to remain at the door because someone must look after the door, to look after a sick child because it must be done ... and so on?

To give the right answer to the questions raised it seems to us that two notions require bringing into prominence once more. In the first place, the notion of the "interior sacrifice", a sacrifice finding its manifold expression in daily life and, finally, its fulfilment in assimilation to the sacrifice of Christ. A passage from St Augustine on this subject, quoted by Fr Bouyer at the end of his book *The Paschal Mystery*, is of capital importance in this context.[6] It can be asserted that this passage, far more than the *Confessions*, inaugurates modern times with the emergence of the human and religious person in the light of God from a society still far too undifferentiated in the objectivism of an insufficiently personalist worship. This passage offers also a true idea of the value of the whole of

[6] The passage in question is from *The City of God*, X, 5-6; see L. Bouyer, *The Paschal Mystery* (London and Chicago, 1951), pp. 329-32.

existence, material and spiritual, at the level of faith and religious life.

But at the other end of the scale to this particular emphasis which can lead to individualism, subjectivism and an undue confusion of sacred and secular, the notion and the reality of the Church as the necessary mediation between man and God needs to be re-emphasized—the Church, the fraternal community outside which (its visible framework and invisible reality being clearly defined) no approach to God is possible.

If these two notions of interior sacrifice and ecclesial community are successfully harmonized, if with some realism we can speak of interior and ecclesial sacrifice, or, if it is preferred, of personalist and sacrificial community, then can be avoided not only all conflict but, also and especially, all danger of falling into those excesses frowned upon by upholders of the liturgy or of the schools of spirituality. Beyond all question it will be seen then that the liturgy occupies a special place in the Church as a manifestation, the only guarantee to the eyes of faith, of personal devotion which she does not reject but, on the contrary, takes for granted at the level of interior sacrifice in its community dimensions and realization.

At this level, it seems clear, the problem raised once more by the booklet by Jacques and Raïssa Maritain, *Liturgy and Contemplation*, a very proper answer to the excesses of a totalitarian liturgism in the devotion and spirituality of the Church, should no longer occur.

PART III

THE PRINCIPAL ADVANCES MADE
BY THE LITURGICAL RENEWAL

CHAPTER VII

THE DIVINE OFFICE

It may be a little paradoxical to begin this third part of the book on the principal advances of the liturgical renewal by speaking of the Divine Office; it has been done because the Office seems to be the least favoured part of the liturgy in this respect, and in this particular lack of emphasis there seems some danger of the whole movement becoming halted at one stage of its development. Speaking quite generally, it can be said that the liturgical renewal has been especially concerned with the Mass, or with the sacraments in general, but has entirely neglected the Office as a whole. Now in this, especially in regard to the faithful, there is serious danger of a too exclusive attachment to eucharistic celebrations, an attach- ment which in the long run must inevitably do harm to these very celebrations. A liturgy which was no longer anything but eucharistic (and that is in practice the case with numerous parishes where there is only Mass—Mass in the morning, at midday, in the evening—and nothing else) is a liturgy doomed to wither because it has thus been separated from the main trunk of the tree of worship whose roots are undeniably in the Divine Office.

The Mass is the flower at the summit of Christian worship. All the rest of Christian worship ought to be comparable to the worship of the synagogue, whence it originated, which con- tinued to be practised by Christ and his apostles, finding in the readings from the Word of God and the singing of the psalms the clearest and commonest of the expressions that they used. And it is only in the practice of this worship that the faith of the congregation will be awakened, educated and nourished to enable them to participate at those times when all the requisite conditions for dignity, all the community dimensions of Christian prayer have been realized, in the eucharistic worship in the proper sense of the term.

The problem of the multiplication of Masses, particularly from the priest's point of view, is not touched on here. We return to it below in speaking of concelebration. Here we mention the problem from its pastoral aspect in view of the devotion of the faithful which we fear to see stunted because it will be reduced not only to the Mass, and cut off from its source of nourishment, but even to the Mass as one practice among others, or in preference to others.

We know, of course, that parish priests often have no choice and that people must be provided for as they come, and that generally means Mass. But to give a somewhat exaggerated picture, perhaps it can be said that in certain cases of the introduction of various methods of participation at Mass (dialogue, commentary etc.), in parishes where the liturgical renewal has taken root, to the ordinary member of the congregation these methods hardly differ from the adoption of some special devotion like the recitation of the Rosary or the introduction of the Nine First Fridays. The faithful indeed show themselves neither silent, surly, nor indifferent, as has too often been asserted, but docile. They have been told that now they must come to Mass rather than to the Rosary or Benediction; they obey and they come. But a time will arrive, and in many places it has already arrived, when presence at Mass, hardly having evolved from being regarded as the fulfilling of an obligation, falls into the routine of what is called religious practice without ever having really been integrated into the personal religious life of the faithful.

It is true that a revival of the Office is faced with very great difficulties which explains, without justifying it, the relative neglect which it has encountered in the liturgical movement. And it may not be out of place to recall at the outset the reaction of the Catholic Counter-Reformation in favour of sacrificial worship in opposition to the simple worship of preaching and the sacrifice of praise of early Protestantism.

In the next place, it is especially to be deplored that so great a confusion has arisen between worship of the Church and monastic worship, on the one hand, and between private recitation and public recitation on the other. It can even be asserted, with some exaggeration it is true, but it brings out more clearly the underlying truth, that even the reforms desired by some are vitiated by this twofold confusion and especially by the second. Thus a reform of the Office, drawn up in the first place with private recitation in view, runs the certain risk of starting on the wrong road at the outset since of its nature the Office, like the Mass, is a community activity and not private, even when in private recitation the intention of the Church comes to supply for the deficiency. A theatrical performance is never arranged on the supposition of there being only one spectator and it would be even more ridiculous to imagine his occupying the theatre all by himself. A theatrical performance is arranged with a full house in view. *Mutatis mutandis*, and granting of course the inadequacy of the comparison between the Office and a play, the process is the same. And indeed it is the same for Mass. No one yet has thought of a liturgical reform based on private celebration. On the contrary, it is agreed by all the promoters of the liturgical revival that Mass in its most solemn form must be envisaged, that is, pontifical high Mass, and that it is on the basis of this form that reforms will be made in the other legitimate types of celebration as required by the circumstances of time and place.[1]

---

[1] It seems not unlikely that the unfavourable reception by some of the new Latin translation of the Psalter was in part due to the fact that the Latin text, an imitation of Ciceronian Latin, hitherto unknown in the liturgical books, was obviously composed with private recitation in view, or, in any case, proved unsuitable for public recitation. The Second Vatican Council has decreed that the work of revising the "Psalter, already happily begun, is to be finished as soon as possible and is to take into account the style of Christian Latin".

Now it is as rearrangements or provisional modifications that the recent changes[2] in the Office have been put forward; they refer principally to private recitation by clerics and, when the occasion arises, by laity. Meanwhile, until the thorough-going reform takes place, and it can hardly do otherwise than take into account various experiments made in different places (hence the importance of paying attention to the non-eucharistic Offices evolved in some communities, groups and parishes) the following *desiderata* mentioned by Cardinal Lercaro at the Assisi Congress are important. It is true, of course, that the new rubrics issued in 1960, and the principles laid down in the liturgical Constitution of the Second Vatican Council carry the modifications in the Breviary further and so bring the Office nearer to the form desired by Cardinal Lercaro, but his fundamental requirements need the full-scale reform of the Breviary promised by the Council and a radical change in outlook on the part of many who use it.

Taking as his starting-point that in a priest's life the Breviary ought to be not a burden but a source of personal and pastoral edification, a privileged task, the *opus Dei* (*psalterium meum, gaudium meum*, as St Augustine said), Cardinal Lercaro raises the problem of the coexistence of private prayer and spiritual exercises on the one hand and public prayer and the Breviary on the other. "The unity of spiritual life has everything to gain from a certain harmonization which would simplify and reduce the burdens and at the same time make more vital the whole apostolic activity of the clergy."[3]

The following points, based on Cardinal Lercaro's paper, are put forward as observations on the present state of affairs combined with suggestions for the future.

1. There must be a real rediscovery of the essential nature of the Office—the sanctification of time, of the hours of the day and of the year; prayer in union with the whole tradition of

---

[2] For a short account of the modifications introduced in the Roman Breviary of recent years see, in this series, *The Liturgical Books* by Lancelot C. Sheppard, pp. 85–108, and chapter XI below.

[3] *MD* 47/48, 299–315.

the Church, Scripture, the writings of the Fathers and Doctors down the ages. This prayer and praise should lead up to the Mass and enable it to be *lived* better.

2. With these points in mind the most urgent need is for the liturgical renewal, which has been centred on the Mass, to take more account of the Office and the need for reform of the Breviary both for the benefit of the clergy and of the laity.

With regard to the clergy, partial reforms of the Breviary have followed one another in the last half century—Pius X, simplification, new distribution of the Psalter, emphasis on the proper of the season; Pius XII, new Latin Psalter, simplification of rubrics; John XXIII, new code of rubrics with greater prominence given to the proper of the season by reform of the calendar and a new classification of feasts. The general trend of this simplification, particularly in the code of rubrics (1960), has been the pastoral emphasis and the return to the fundamental idea of the Office as the sanctification of time. The special prominence given to the temporal Office with a reduction of the sanctoral is also noteworthy. The liturgical Constitution of the Second Vatican Council has legislated for a reform of the Breviary

What will be its principal points? There will certainly be a further reduction of the length of the Office by distribution of the Psalms over a longer period and the suppression in private recitation, perhaps, of what is specifically intended for choral celebration, a rearrangement and refashioning of the lectionary, with, certainly, further prominence given to the Office of the Season[4] and the suppression of feasts which celebrate an "idea" rather than an "event". This indeed has been the general trend since Pius X's reform in 1911.

With regard to the laity, certain steps have been taken which, though they have not yet received that official sanction which is

---

[4] While the 1960 rubrics go a long way in giving prominence to the Office of the Season, particularly of Advent and Lent, the point has not yet been reached outside these two seasons where it can be said that the the ferial Office is the rule rather than the exception. It remains to be seen how far the reform of the Breviary promised in the Constitution on Liturgy of the Second Vatican Council will affect the calendar.

required to make them fully liturgical, are worth noting here. A great number of Breviaries for lay people have been published in all languages. In English there are *The Short Breviary* (published by St John's Abbey, Collegeville) and *The Little Breviary* (London, 1958). Yet these lay Offices "raise a problem. Should the Office for the laity be fashioned on the model of that used by the clergy?" asks Cardinal Lercaro. Here again it seems that practice must decide and that the most successful examples will attract the attention of those entrusted with the reform of the Breviary who will thus be in a position to obtain the necessary official sanction. In any case, what is to be aimed at is the further (and normal) stage when, as at Mass, the Office, taking into account the present way of life among civilized peoples and the daily timetable of the active population, gathers together clergy and faithful for the praise of God and the hearing of his word.

CHAPTER VIII

THE LITURGICAL RENEWAL AND THE EUCHARIST

In the context of this third part of the book no mention is made of the advances achieved in theology as a result of the liturgical movement—biblical theology, the theology of the mystery of worship—since something has already been said of these matters in the second part. Here, on the subject of the Eucharist, we are concerned rather to detail a number of practical improvements with reference, not to understanding of the holy Sacrifice, but to its celebration. These improvements, none the less, are derived so directly from theological considerations that it is impossible not to refer to them summarily by way of introduction and as positive contributions made by the liturgical renewal.

Since the whole liturgical movement started from a rediscovery of the tradition of the Church, and more specially still from a rediscovery, not to say a discovery purely and simply, of the theology of the Church, the same holds good, right at the outset, for the Eucharist as sacrifice and sacrament. Thus, looking at the question on the level of theory, the direct inspiration of practice, the latter being the soil in which the former is made fruitful, we feel that at the present time the key to eucharistic worship is to be found in a better grasp of the relationship between Mass as a sacrament and Mass as a sacrifice, a relationship expressed in its simplest form as Mass-sacrificial meal.

It may well be asked why Christ chose bread and wine to symbolize and make effective his presence among us. If this presence was the ultimate purpose of his sacred institution, the transubstantiated bread and wine being reduced in fact to mere appearances, would it not have been better if his choice had fallen on a pearl, which does not corrupt or decay, or on a perfume, a more pervasive element, which would have rendered his presence more durable or more significant?

If Christ chose bread and wine it was, it seems, to show, at a given stage in civilization by the help of these elements of human communion, that by which his disciples could show and perpetuate the essence of his sacrifice. If, in fact, it is the essence of this sacrifice to be a total gift of absolute oblation to his Father, it can be said that Christ found no better way of expressing this divine gift than by means of elements which manifest, signify and effect a mutual gift among men. This can be said shortly by stating that Christ found perhaps no better expression of divine charity than human charity, since the latter is evidence of the former and is at the same time its consequence. In this way Christ reduced the twofold commandment of the Law to one alone.

That seems to be the meaning of the Johannine account of the Last Supper. Omitting the narrative of the institution, and in some sort substituting for it the account of the washing of feet as a gesture of friendly and brotherly welcome on the part of God himself, it dwells at length on the commandment of love among the disciples in relation to the revelation of the three divine Persons. This is also the meaning of the Pauline account which includes the institution narrative in a purely ecclesial context of love shared in daily life. And it is probably for the same reason that at this moment Luke inserts the dispute which arose between the disciples on the subject of who was greatest among them. In any case, it is the realization of two logia related by the Synoptics: "It is mercy that wins favour with me, not sacrifice," and "Where two or three are gathered together in my name, I am there in the midst of them".

Setting aside the former types of sacrifice in Judaism and the practices of worship surrounding them, Christ effectively reduced the worship of the new Alliance to the existence of the ecclesial community as such, as brotherly love: this love was both the witness and presence of Christ as the personified and incarnate expression of divine love, a love coming from God and given back to him in the highest way on the cross.

It is this which makes the Mass essential communion, though this does not mean that the essence of sacrifice is confined to and is effected at the precise moment that bears this name, when the sacred species are consumed by the celebrant and the congregation. Rather is it all the Mass that is communion, in the gathering together of the congregation and the attitudes which manifest it, in the hearing of the Word and in the common expression of praise—all being accomplished over the bread and wine offered as symbols of this constant communion (this appears very clearly in the *Didache*). And the consecration is then the supreme moment of this brotherly communion which causes it to pass from symbol to reality. It is the moment when God answers fully the expectations of his faithful people in communion. It is the moment when God consecrates this brotherly communion by giving himself in his Son, really present under the species which make the communion manifest and effect the marvellous exchange, and the still more marvellous union, between this human brotherly love and its fulfilment in divine love by Christ, who is this Love in person.

And so there are no longer two loves. Just as substantially the bread and wine have disappeared, the brotherly communion which they symbolize is entirely merged in Christ's offering as a victim, the supreme expression of divine love, made really present on the altar under the species of bread and wine and at the precise moment of communion in the hearts of the faithful who share them. The "assumption" and as it were the "absorption" of the physical and human matter of the sacrifice are thus total. It is like the heat of the water mingled with the chalice after the consecration in the Byzantine rite, or like the fire from heaven which consumed the sacrifice of the prophet Elias. These symbols represent the real presence of Christ at Mass and the manner which, in him, priest and victim at the same time, God incarnate assuming in his person his whole mystical body, the love of God totally integrates the love of creation. The latter, in the communion of men with each other, is a figure here below, as nearly as it is possible for it to be, of the circumincession of the divine Persons which make them one in the holy Trinity.

This way of putting matters seems to place Trinitarian unity and ecclesial unity in a real and vital relationship in the sacrifice-meal and communion. It is founded on several scriptural contexts and is represented by a considerable tradition from the *Didache* to St Augustine.

This is also the way in which worship and life can be really coordinated, since worship, in accordance with the twofold commandment of love reduced to unity, is the sacred moment of life passed in charity—the special work of the disciples of Jesus and their *opus Dei*.

It is also the way really to explain, and not merely to acknowledge, the primitive and traditional doctrine of the common priesthood of the faithful, an idea so fundamental that, as Jungmann has shown, the terms which properly designate the priesthood were only used in the first two centuries in speaking of Christ or of the whole Church. We see here that the common priesthood of the faithful in the unity of the Church is not only a juridical function for the celebration of the sacrifice, it is, as mutual consent, brotherly communion before God, "body and soul" of the sacrament which, by the real presence, becomes the efficacious sign of divine love.

In the last place, to come to the real purpose of these considerations, it is what explains, at the starting-point of the liturgical movement, Pius X's insistence on *active* participation. If it is not just one method like another, laid down by the pope for the purpose of obtaining a better, technically more perfect celebration of the Eucharist, it must be thought that it goes much further and comes very near to the very essence of the Eucharist as ecclesial and Christocentric significant communion, in the sense of *ex opere operato*, of divine grace.

This participation and its most external forms of expression come near, according to the intention of the Church, to the very essence of the sacrifice-sacrament. And the active participation of the faithful, as of the celebrant and his ministers, in eucharistic worship is a way which is significant in itself of what this worship really effects. If such active participation is not absolutely required for validity, since one communicant, namely the celebrant, can by intention represent all the others (although the traditional insistence on the presence of at least a server is significant in this respect) it is no less evident that this validity itself requires active, congregational participation *in voto*, as every properly liturgical act is, *in voto*, an act of the whole Church. The need for participation by the congregation could not have been put more plainly than it is in the liturgical Constitution of the Second Vatican Council. In it participation (internal as well as external) is seen to be an essential part of public worship; indeed the reform of the books of the Roman rite is to be carried out with such participation in view so that the congregation may take part *scienter, actuose et fructuose*— that is, their participation is to be informed, active and fruitful.

This explains, without fully justifying it, the repugnance of some of the clergy for what are called "private" Masses,[1] and it is this, too, which inspires their desire for a return to the ancient custom, still practised in the Eastern Church, of concelebration. They are not, of course, thereby calling in question the legitimacy or the value of individual celebration, according to the circumstances of time and place (see below).

This whole way of rethinking and reordering the mystery of worship, cannot, without injustice, be taxed with a hankering after novelty, or with archeologism. It is certainly, and in the

---

[1] The new rubrics of the Roman Missal lay down that the expression "private Mass" is to be avoided: *Denominatio proinde Missae privatae vitetur* (n. 269).

present case indeed to a high degree, an authentic way of thinking with the Church, *sentire cum Ecclesia*. It is a question of the authentic expression in the very method of celebration, and in accordance with the sacramental order, of what it is really to effect. And that is brotherly communion in the name of Christ, the efficacious sign of his real presence as God's answer made to man—to man who, following Christ's example, in the unity of fellowship seeks God and finds him as a Father.

This renewal of the quest for eucharistic authenticity, which should find its counterpart in daily life, particularly in the practice of charity and of the missionary ideal, is in any case what appears to emerge most clearly from all that has been done at the practical, external level of eucharistic celebrations. It is now time to deal with this aspect of the question. In the following explanation account has been taken of the various episcopal directives for Mass as well as of the principal practices at the parochial level which these same directives have sanctioned. All that is said here is valid, *mutatis mutandis* of every kind of liturgical gathering, but it refers particularly to the Mass. And it is for this reason that it finds a place in this chapter.

PRINCIPAL INNOVATIONS OR REFORMS

The altar

The part played by the altar in the celebration and the doctrine concerning it need to be explained. The altar should stand free with its surroundings unencumbered. Its rôle as sacrificial table, particularly, should appear with the greatest possible clarity.[2]

The celebrant

The correctness, dignity and even elegance of the celebrant's gestures and attitudes are not superfluous extras. Like the altar, the celebrant, who really presides over the congregation, and is Christ's representative, must stand out clearly. Thus

[2] Cf. *MD* 51, 132–45.

those Masses are inadmissible at which another priest from the pulpit, or from the middle of the nave, superimposes on the entire Mass an obtrusive commentary, relegating the celebrant to the background.

The commentator (and other diaconal functions)

Increasingly, while the usefulness of a commentary is admitted, its great dangers are coming to be recognized. It can easily lead to lack of reverence, distraction of attention from the centre of the celebration (priest and altar), and hindrance to prayer. The following proposals have been put forward.

Greater recourse should be had to instruction outside Mass than to instruction during Mass.

Properly speaking, the term "commentary" during Mass should not be used; it is preferable to talk of "monition", on the pattern of what was done by the deacon in the early Church. In other words, there should be a summons to prayer, in sober language, unadorned, obviously suggesting a motive for prayer in accordance with the mystery celebrated. But this motive should never be an explanation; it should lead immediately to prayer and should itself be couched in the form of a prayer.

Especially must care be taken to avoid any drowning of the celebrant's voice, or coming between celebrant and congregation, as was mentioned above; the collects must not be duplicated, but should be prepared for by a monition which will be separated from the collect said by the celebrant by a period of silence as is observed in the Good Friday liturgy and other of the ancient Masses between *Flectamus genua* and *Levate*. The period of silence is for the congregation to give interior expression to its intentions which are afterwards "resumed" by the celebrant in the collect.

As a general rule the monitions should be read from a previously prepared text; this is not to prevent all improvisation but to help the "deacon" to direct his fervour into the proper channel, for he too must really take part in the celebration without forgetting that all liturgy implies a certain hieratic style.

The congregation

As Fr Bouyer has shown, for a long time the idea of liturgy as a spectacle, like the grandiose ceremonies of the seventeenth-century French court, was everywhere current. We are in course of rediscovering nowadays that the liturgy is the work of the people, that there are not actors and "audience" since the congregation is in itself "mystery" of Christ.

From this general principle, which has been recalled and developed several times already in the course of this book, the following conclusions emerge:

The first way in which the congregation takes part is that it has gathered together. The primary quality of its participation, therefore, is to be found in the way that it has assembled. Its very material disposition should manifest its unity. But so far as possible (and this is a serious problem for huge urban parishes) this unity should be able to manifest itself by the parish Mass which should be the high Mass. Here we encounter the difficulty of several Masses; we shall refer to it again. There is also to be noted the danger of reserving the parish high Mass, either by reason of its inconvenient time or its archaic character, or else because even the clergy are not enthusiastic about it, to a handful of habitués scattered about the church—pensioners, old ladies who have already communicated at the seven o'clock Mass, sisters from the neighbouring home or institution who have already had their community Mass.

Total participation of the congregation is effected by sacramental communion. Hence the mitigation of the eucharistic fast and the recommendation that communion should be given from hosts consecrated during the Mass in question, as the Encyclical *Mediator* and the Constitution on liturgy of the Second Vatican Council requires; hence, too, the solemnization of communion by means of a procession and congregational singing.

Participation is also to be found in the ordinary attitudes in church which enable the congregation to live the mystery celebrated and knit them together in unity. The education of the congregation in these matters is always necessary. But care must be taken very patiently to offer reasons for the directions given regarding the attitudes to be adopted for the different parts of the Mass. It may be pointed out in this connection that the normal attitude for Christian prayer is standing; beginning with our Lady at the foot of the cross, it was the attitude of the early Christians. The celebrant at the altar always stands. It is important to observe, also, that apart from the aged and the sick, it is the attitude that can be asked of the congregation with the least difficulty.

Participation is expressed also by the singing and the responses of the congregation. The schola or choir ought not to prevent the faithful from making the responses or from singing. Its function is to execute certain anthems that the congregation does not know and it is legitimate on occasion for the latter to listen (there are certain meditative chants, like the gradual, which are intended for this purpose). In addition, it is the function of the schola to sustain the singing of the congregation, but it ought not to take the place of the congregation or require it to sing pieces that are too difficult.

In addition to these arrangements concerning attitudes, singing and responses, there are a certain number of laws governing the congregation which confer on it its own essential nature. They are here described summarily:

1. The Christian congregation is in the first place a festive gathering. Joy is a necessary condition of a liturgy and of a liturgical congregation; all forms of celebration share to a certain extent in the paschal joy in expectation of the Kingdom.

2. The Christian congregation is hierarchical. It forms a sort of symphony in which there are different parts. "And this is not merely to prevent confusion and disorder; it is rather, the direct consequence of the fact that the Church, the *ecclesia*, does not meet on its own initiative, or because its members have spontaneously gathered together, but rather because it has

been convoked by God's Word, speaking to it in the manner befitting that Word."[3]

3. Proclamation and hearing of the Word of God. "The reading of the Scripture that takes place in the framework of the Mass is not merely one among many types of reading the divine Word; it is the chief and fundamental type to which all the others refer as to their norm. And, to penetrate still more deeply into this truth, it is in the living liturgical celebration alone, with all that this celebration . . . implies for the living Church, that God's Word can be accepted as it desires to be accepted."[4]

4. Prayer. "The readings of the synagogal service and, still earlier, all the proclamations of the Word of God, have always been connected with the people's prayer and praise."[5]

5. The offering of the people in the one only sacrifice of Christ. "In this thanksgiving, the whole story of the redemption of Israel as proclaimed in the Bible was summed up in praise, the people thus created by God were dedicated anew to him, and a petition was made for a future and final intervention of God by which he would accomplish the work he had begun and himself bring to perfection the offering of the People."[6]

6. The Christian congregation is, in the last place, communion, as we have sufficiently shown at the beginning of this chapter. Here it need merely be recalled with Jungmann that the rôle of the congregation amounts to removing the veil of mist that in the later Middle Ages came down between the people in the nave and the worship at the altar. The faithful must realize that they are not strangers and sojourners, still less are they mere spectators of what Christ effects at the altar through the ministry of the priest. "The liturgy is the worship rendered by the mystical Body of Christ in the entirety of its Head and members."

[3] L. Bouyer, *Liturgy and Life* (American edn, *Liturgical Piety*), p. 32.
[4] *Ibid.*, pp. 30–1.
[5] *Ibid.*, p. 115.
[6] *Ibid.*, pp. 115–16.

We give here an example of a celebration in the seventeenth century as a conclusion to this section on the rôle of the congregation. We are concerned here with the hero discovered by Fr Bouyer. His name was Jubé. In him we could see a precursor, if he had not gone much further than our own liturgical renewal, or even a prophet, if his example did not inspire with considerable modesty more than one contemporary liturgist.

The most famous among those liturgical pioneers of the seventeenth century was later denounced by Dom Guéranger as having been a living combination of heresies of all kinds, although, as a matter of fact, he can only be reproached for having signed the Appeal against the Bull *Unigenitus*, as did many of the most respectable churchmen of the time. This pioneer's name was Jubé, and he was the parish priest of Asnières, at that period a small place near Paris on the west bank of the Seine. Jubé insisted first of all on the public and collective character of the Mass. As a consequence, he never used the high altar in his church except on Sundays and feastdays when the congregation gathered together. He also restored the old Roman usage (which had endured longer in France than in Rome itself) of placing the linen cloth on the altar only just before Mass, and of having no other cross or lights on the altar than the processional cross and tapers, which were set in place at the beginning of Mass. Jubé began Mass by saying the Psalm *Judica* and the *Confiteor* along with the people; then he sat down at the Epistle side of the altar and listened to the Epistle and Gospel as they were sung by the assistant ministers, after having sung the collect himself. He sang the *Kyrie*, *Gloria* and *Credo* along with the people, instead of saying them in a low voice by himself. He also restored the offertory procession, (which had never entirely disappeared from French churches), and had offerings of all kinds made in this procession which he later blessed at the *Per quem haec omnia* at the end of the canon, according to the original practice. He never began the canon before the *Sanctus* had been sung in full and he said the prayers of the canon loudly enough to be heard by the whole congregation in his small church. In other words, he wanted once more to make the readings, the singing, the prayers, the offertory real, rather than merely conventional acts; and he wanted to have the sacrifice offered with the full, though always hierarchically ordered, participation of the Christian people. Dom Guéranger later regarded all these practices of Jubé as so many reasons for horror and dismay. But we of today can see in most of them intelligent and healthy improvements, had they been introduced with the consent of proper authority.[7]

THE QUESTION OF CONCELEBRATION

The best introduction to this subject is that written by Dom Lambert Beauduin.[8] He establishes in the first place the legitimacy of the rite, taking into account the reservations of the canons and despite the discussions which took place on this subject in the later Middle Ages. And he shows what is the fundamental underlying theological idea; the unity of the priesthood which is made visible by this rite grouping around the bishop, the sole depositary of the fullness of the priesthood of the eternal Pontiff, the whole diocesan community, according to their various hierarchical functions. A third paragraph sketches the historical tradition, especially at Rome, down to the giving up of the rite by the Western Church towards the end of the thirteenth century. Finally, noting the various traces of the practice still remaining, he respectfully expresses the desire for a restoration of concelebration which is so expressive of the Catholic spirit. That desire has now been granted by the liturgical Constitution promulgated on December 4th, 1963. Reference is made to this in the last chapter of this book, but it may be useful to mention here, however, certain matters which, although elementary, are too little known, and certain questions of a practical nature.

In the first place, it should be remembered that until a relatively late date (fourth century) there was only one Mass in Rome and that was the pope's; again, in St Thomas Aquinas's time, it was forbidden for two Masses to be celebrated at the same time in a church; that at the present time in the Byzantine

[7] *Ibid.*, pp. 53–4.
[8] See *MD* 7.

rite it is forbidden for two Masses to be celebrated at the same altar on the same day and that, if the practice of concelebration, in this and other oriental rites, is not usual it is entirely allowed and recognized; finally, that in the Roman rite there is concelebration at ordination Masses and at those of the consecration of a bishop, and that on Maundy Thursday only one Mass is celebrated in a church at which priests and faithful communicate.

It is true that with this last tradition, in fact evacuated of its substance, if it can be put thus, since there is no concelebration in the proper sense of the term by the priests, but only communion, can be compared the custom whereby a priest is allowed to celebrate three Masses on All Souls day and Christmas day. It can certainly be pointed out that it is here a question of permission (three Masses may be celebrated) whereas in the other case there is prohibition (it is forbidden on Maundy Thursday, as a general rule, to celebrate any other Mass than the community Mass). But this consideration would certainly not suffice to establish the principle of the multiplication of Masses and their frequency, and it is here that the real difficulty occurs.

What in fact is the reason that a priest celebrates one or several Masses, or that he does not celebrate at all in order to communicate and concelebrate? Is it the devotion of the priest and can one take as an example the case of the pope who celebrated several times a day, or the holy Jesuit priest who obtained an indult so that he could make his Mass last an hour and a half in order to satisfy his eucharistic devotion? Can it be the infinite value of the sacrifice of the Mass? But is this value, which in fact is infinite, since it is derived from the sacrifice consummated once for all upon the cross, subject to numerical considerations, to arithmetical calculations? If it is, why do not priests, whose principal function is to offer Mass, divest themselves of other obligations, to be able to celebrate several times a day and thus increase to the maximum number, as their devotion would lead them to do, the number of Masses celebrated uninterruptedly on earth?

We can see from these simple questions that considerations of devotion and those which take into account the infinite value of the Mass are not a sufficient explanation of the multiplication of Masses. To put it more accurately, they cannot establish a norm for their frequency. How then can this be done?

In the absence of a clear and quick answer to unravel this complicated question a little, it can be advanced, firstly, that it is better provisionally to leave aside certain related questions like the precept obliging the faithful and priests to be present at Mass or to celebrate, the merits accruing to the celebration of Mass or presence at it and, *a fortiori*, the question of stipends. These questions are by no means secondary, but are nevertheless placed second in the sense that they ought not to influence the solution otherwise than as indications and should owe the recognition that they obtain to the fact that the question has already been solved.

In the next place, it is important to recall the difference of the "traditions" in the Church and their unequal value, not to mention their relative authenticity. In addition to Tradition (with a capital letter) and those traditions which are its expression at the dogmatic level, it is essential to place in their proper category those customs of a canonical and liturgical nature, sanctioned by usage and canon law, especially when, in another part of the Church, contrary customs are also legitimately established; in this way we shall cease to do wrong to our brethren in the faith and the same ecclesial communion by regarding as merely tolerated, or even as abuses, their customs which are contrary to our own.

Looking indeed at those customs and practices which are our own, we must take greater care to separate the chaff from the wheat. Thus it would have been possible to urge against Pius X's institution of frequent communion and that of children a "tradition" of many centuries standing in the opposite sense. In truth, it was not a tradition but rather the loss of the understanding of the tradition which has now been made clear, or more serious still, a lack of normal and necessary development in the life of the Church.

With these considerations in mind, it seems that to find a norm for the frequency of the celebration of Mass we must consider the eucharistic mystery as a whole. The principles established at the beginning of the present chapter can here be of some help to us. They amounted, in short, to bringing out clearly the essential link between what signifies and what is signified; what signifies is fundamentally the ecclesial community gathered together for the breaking of bread and symbolized before the consecration by the bread and wine as elements of communion; what is signified is the divine love which, in the Person of Christ made present on the altar at the moment of consecration, assumes and transfigures the communion in fellowship of the Church gathered together in his name.

If that is true it seems obvious that the ancient practice, shown by having only one Mass and by concelebration, is nearer to the primitive institution and the structure on which it is founded. The fact of the gathering together of the community being an essential in what signifies, it seems that the frequency of Mass ought to be regulated, in principle, on this. In practice account would be taken of legitimately related elements.

If then in a particular place the whole congregation can be gathered together for a Mass, this will be the Mass and there will be only one. And the Mass will be celebrated as often as reasonably and with due dignity the community can be gathered anew. Thus what has hitherto been precept could also become the norm. The Sunday precept could also be the norm for the parochial celebration as the custom of conventual Mass could be the norm of the frequency of celebration in a community of monastic type. In that case it would be necessary to be very careful to determine not only the types of community but their real diversification. It is certain that at the present time, within the boundaries of an urban parish, there are in fact several communities. It can be said indeed that there are as many parish communities as there are Masses. In ecclesiastical parlance it is common to hear mention of the "eleven o'clock congregation".

And in fact these are different sections of the public that require to be sociologically determined and to be integrated afresh in the unity of the community and of the parochial Mass. In this respect the multiplicity of Masses in a parish will no longer be a derogation to the principle, any more than the existence of these Masses is in relation to the bishop's Mass.

A similar procedure would make it easy to determine the frequency of Masses during the week and Masses for special groups. In this respect the decree on evening Masses contains certain useful indications. On the other hand, the celebration of "private" Masses apart from, and *a fortiori* during community celebrations, as well as the multiplicity of Masses in a monastery, raises a real problem and it seems that if this problem is to be solved by concelebration it is equally true that a necessary preliminary is the solution of the problem of the multiplication of the priestly office, according to the needs of places and periods. But that is another problem.

As a conclusion to this section, and in case one point or another raised above has been misunderstood, there is added here a word on the solitary Eucharist. It is obvious, indeed, that a celebration in isolation is not *per se* implicated in what was said above since it was put forward as a suggestion on the norm to be established for the frequency of Masses. This will easily be seen from the following comparison between celebration by a priest who is a passenger on a liner and celebration by Fr de Foucauld in the desert. Many priests have had experience of celebration on board ship, especially with pilgrimage groups when there are several priests present. Conditions, it can be said, are, at the very least, summary. On the other hand, it is certain that the intention of the isolated celebrant makes up for the significance of the ecclesial congregation. But more than that, in the case of Fr de Foucauld in the Sahara or of Fr Peyriguère in the Berber mountains, or again in the case of a priest explorer in the Arabian desert or Central Asia, the intention of the priest celebrating with the whole Church and in her name assumes an entirely different meaning. In the name of the universal Church, he celebrates, alone, for that local Church which only exists in himself. And this can be true also of an isolated priest in a Christian country as in missionary territory. In the suburbs of a great dechristianized city, or in the depths of the country, it can be said that, following the diversity and the impenetrability of classes and peoples, the priest by himself is the Church. And his Eucharist is then in a very special way what indeed it is, the desire, previously expressed by fasting, of a divine presence which in the end will triumph over human impenetrability and obtain, by virtue of the words of the Gospel, perfect union of strangers and sojourners in the humanity of Jesus, priest and victim. This solitary Eucharist is then like that which is celebrated in brotherly union with a soul in danger, in the keen suffering of being unable to share with this soul the eucharistic communion. It is the bread of fellowship which is then broken and the fact that it is eaten alone does not impair within us the desire for others, a loved one or some special section of humanity, the sustenance of the essential desire for God and for his kingdom, *donec veniat.*

A religious who for long years experienced the fact of the Eucharist in solitude can express far better than we can these things and restore for us, if we have lost them, the legitimacy and the profound meaning of such solitary celebrations. Fr Charles-André Poissonier, a Franciscan hermit at Tazert in South Morocco, who died in 1938 and was an almost immediate disciple of Fr de Foucauld, wrote in his private notebook:

When I celebrate Mass alone in my little chapel which on one side dominates Tazert and on the other clings to the mountainside in which it is embedded; when at night I recite my Office alone with our Lord present before me, it is then that I feel, it is then that I live my missionary life, for it is in the name of all those surrounding me that I pray, that I adore, that I render to God the homage due to him. As I have in some sort become a Moroccan, by my incorporation among this people with whom I live in close relations, and on the other hand, having become a member of Christ by my faith, I have the impression that in me Christ has become a Moroccan and desires to pray himself for his Moroccan brothers. It is in that especially that I feel myself to be a missionary, far more than in my medical work which is and must remain secondary. And so it is of little importance if the harvest is not yet even beginning to grow, if perhaps, and even probably, I shall not see it with my eyes. I shall nevertheless have fulfilled my missionary rôle by bringing the prayer of Christ to a place where it was not hitherto.... Christ will have taken possession of a part of his Kingdom which he did not previously possess....

In another context Pierre Teilhard de Chardin said the same thing no less admirably in "The Mass on the world" (see at the end of *The Milieu divin*).

CHAPTER IX

PASTORAL PRACTICE AND
THE SACRAMENTS

FUNDAMENTAL REQUIREMENTS

Ever since the Council of Trent, and in reaction against Protestant moralism, Catholic theology has felt itself obliged to insist on the principle of *opus operatum*. But if, from this point of view, it is true that in the celebration of Mass or the administration of the sacraments, "one priest is as good as another", from the canonical point of view the problem of validity does not exclude that of licitness. It must also be remembered that the spiritual movement of the post-Tridentine period was concerned far more greatly than in previous times to promote a sacerdotal spirituality, to insist, that is, on the moral and religious dispositions of the minister of the sacraments and of the celebrant of the Eucharist. And yet it is true, perhaps, that until recently less consideration was given to the pastoral problem raised by the dispositions of the faithful. The first important sign of a renewal in this field is to be found, probably, at the beginning of this century in the measures taken by Pius X for the promotion of frequent communion and the admission of children to the holy table. It required this action of the supreme authority for Christian people no longer to regard themselves as excommunicated to all intents and purposes. The movement thus set on foot by Pius X forms the starting-point for a more acute awareness of all that is required of us by the sacrament that is offered to us.

It is clear in fact that our faith in the *opus operatum* of the sacraments in no wise allays the uneasiness that we experience when confronted by those who from routine, or from an attachment, founded on a species of folklore rather than on faith, to ceremonies whose real significance has been lost to sight, continue to have recourse to the priest for the baptism of their children and for marriage. It is difficult to ascertain how far genuine faith subsists beneath this quasi-superstitious attachment to traditional institutions. It could be the still smoking flax that we must be careful not to quench. But obviously that is not enough. The question is to discover what can be done to revive the flame and bring these nominal Christians to an understanding of what in the eyes of the Church is the meaning of the act that they ask of her.

The primary concern will therefore be to lead those who thus present themselves for the reception of a sacrament to dispositions of actual faith. The Council of Trent, and those who worked to render effective the reform that it promulgated, attached great importance to children's catechism. But at a dechristianized period like our own the problem of the instruction of adults has become increasingly urgent. Since some of those who still ask the Church to bless their marriages and baptize their children scarcely ever go to Mass and are thus deprived of the instruction that is given in the liturgy of the Word, it can hardly be considered strange to wonder what is the real significance for them of the marriage or the baptism that they ask of the Church.

In those countries where these religious acts are quite distinct from the corresponding civil formalities it would seem to be relatively easy to make it clear to people that these sacraments have in fact no significance other than a religious one. And so on these occasions a purely administrative attitude must be avoided; the priest must not confine himself merely to registering a baptism or a marriage but take the trouble to make these events the basis of a real adult catechesis.

So far as marriage is concerned, the increasingly precise canonical prescriptions regarding the preliminary inquiries provide the priest, responsible for this investigation, with the basis for instruction, which must lead those with whom he is dealing to a realization that they are not undergoing a tiresome formality, but that they can obtain real spiritual benefit from this living contact with their pastor. And he, provided that he does not lose sight of the spirit informing the letter of the regulations, can be led to a genuine concern for the religious education of the betrothed couple who come to him.

In this way new institutions arise to meet new needs. Retreats are organized for engaged couples and even a sort of catechumenate during which a series of instructions is spread over a fairly long period. Aid is sought from various quarters, from doctors, from couples with some experience of married life. In short, the dialogue between priest and faithful is broadened to the dimension of the Christian community, of an institution of the Church in which each individual according to his own particular competence, his own particular gifts, has his positive contribution to offer. By his presence the priest must ensure that these meetings become real liturgies, preparing for the sacramental liturgy which is now incorporated with the baptismal liturgy.

Moreover, the whole of the fervent community must be concerned with those whose faith is obscured by prejudice and misunderstandings and should strive to lead them, especially on the occasion of marriage, to clearer awareness of the Gospel message that perhaps they have not troubled to study since childhood. For this purpose, systematic explanations of the Christian faith have been organized, in addition to the special preparation for marriage, for those who have come to this important turning-point of their vocation.

Something of the same sort should be done for baptisms. If the practice of infant baptism can be justified by the principle of *opus operatum*, from the pastoral point of view a real catechumenate ought to be instituted for the benefit of the parents and godparents who have taken the step of asking for baptism for a child. It can take shape quite naturally by informal instructions, visits to families, etc., and normally should last some time according to the needs of the Christian education of the neophyte, until the age when he can regularly attend catechism lessons. In this way baptism will no longer be a mere formality and the occasion of a celebration that is entirely of worldly inspiration; thus too, the primary meaning of the baptismal liturgy can be rediscovered by those who previously were present at its rites as passive spectators without seeking to understand their meaning.

Something like two years before the voting of the Constitution on liturgy at the Second Vatican Council the Congregation of Rites gave permission for the rite of baptism of adults to be performed in stages during the instruction of the convert. This virtual restoration of the catechumenate has been followed by the instruction in the Constitution on liturgy of the Second Vatican Council which lays down that "the catechumenate for adults is to be restored; it is to comprise several distinct steps, and to be taken into use as and when the Ordinary may see fit".

Lastly, the same concern for adult catechesis is to be found in assistance of the sick and dying. By instructing the faithful about the real meaning of the prayers of the Church and the rites of the sacrament of the sick the priest will combat the prevailing prejudice about this sacrament and accustom Christians no longer to regard it as the sacrament of the dying but as an appeal to God for the recovery of the sick person: "Stretch out your right hand and set him on his feet again, put strength into him, and keep him safe under your powerful protection, give him back again to your holy Church..." (liturgy of the sick).

In this way by a concern to lead the candidate for the sacraments to dispositions of faith an attempt will be made to make the sacrament intelligible. Bilingual rituals have already been adopted in many countries. Obviously, when it is a question of certain rites which have, so to say, become a trifle stale in the course of time under the influence of routine or misunderstood practical necessities, the matter is one of some delicacy. Thus the exorcisms at baptism have not been translated in the bilingual rituals in English-speaking countries. But it is clear that there is a problem here. In the Nestorian Church the exorcisms have been eliminated from the baptismal liturgy; this, in the view of all other Christian Churches of East and West, is the effect of the Pelagian heresy, whose influence, rejected everywhere else, has been successful among Nestorians. In the state of mind provoked by the liturgical movement we shall experience increasingly, no doubt, a rediscovery of those values of faith which formed the foundation of all our traditional rites, and increasingly, too, we shall apreciate their authentic savour. Now that the whole ritual of the sacraments, including the sacramental forms, may be in the vernacular and the rites themselves are to be reformed as a result of the liturgical Constitution, this rediscovery and greater appreciation are likely to be easier and to occur more quickly.

THE SACRAMENTS AND THE PASCHAL MYSTERY

The liturgical reform of the Easter vigil is undoubtedly one of the most important events of the history of the liturgical renewal. From the outset it was allowed to incorporate in it the administration of baptism which gives its full significance to this vigil. The present liturgy provides that all the faithful should be associated with this baptismal emphasis by a solemn renewal each year on this occasion of their baptismal promises and profession of faith; this allusion to baptism is maintained even in the case when there is no neophyte in the congregation.

As we know, in the time of St Augustine certain considerations caused the administration of baptism to be postponed until after the age of reason and even until adulthood, thus prolonging the catechumenate throughout youth, except of course in danger of death when baptism was always given to infants. Thus there is a certain opposition between considerations of a pedagogical nature and those of a theological nature which urge that children should be admitted at an early age not only to baptism but to the fullness of sacramental life according to the custom that has been preserved in the Churches of the East.

The same opposition between the pedagogical and theological points of view is encountered again with confirmation. In the traditional enumeration of the sacraments we begin by mentioning the three sacraments of Christian initiation which formerly were all three conferred during the Easter vigil—baptism, confirmation, Eucharist—and this is still the Eastern custom. In the Latin Church, since confirmation as a general rule is normally reserved to the bishop, more often than not there would be an insurmountable practical difficulty in including it in the Easter vigil. On the other hand, if it is more normal, from the theological point of view, to confer confirmation before first Communion, from the pedagogical point of view there is a temptation to postpone the age of confirmation which is here regarded as the sacrament of Christian maturity. This is the custom which has become fairly well established in the Protestant Churches. In fact, among most Catholics confirmation does not stand out very clearly. The liturgical Constitution of the Second Vatican Council has, however, made it clear that confirmation forms part of the rites of Christian initiation and has said that it may be given within Mass when convenient. The rite is to be revised in order to show the "intimate connection of this sacrament with the whole process of Christian initiation" and to make it emerge more clearly; for the same reason, the Constitution continues, it is fitting that "candidates should renew their baptismal promises just before they are confirmed".

At the end of the Middle Ages, and in the seventeenth and eighteenth centuries in most Western countries, the point was reached of omitting entirely to confer confirmation. The present practice of the Catholic Church is in sharp reaction against such a tendency, but if, in practice, all children are confirmed and the present law of the Church even allows all parish priests to administer the sacrament to children of school age in danger of death, it certainly cannot be said that this sacrament is better understood and stands out more clearly in the memories of the majority of Christians. We have here, then, a concrete situation, which will no doubt call for further development since, in the prevailing climate of the liturgical renewal it is increasingly felt to be abnormal.

In any case, the restoration of the Easter vigil to its fundamental and primary significance has made a valuable contribution to showing more clearly the community character of the sacraments conferred on this occasion.

PENANCE

The sacrament of penance gave every appearance at one time of being the indisputable condition for the reception of communion. In the stages of a child's religious life the following steps were commonly regarded as usual—baptism, penance, Eucharist, confirmation. This was an order very different from the traditional order of the sacraments which preserves the idea of the unity of the three sacraments of Christian initiation, the sacrament of penance only being mentioned afterwards, together with the sacrament of the sick, which was regarded in a similar way.

Under the influence of the liturgical renewal, and especially of the practice of frequent communion, which has increasingly restored among the faithful the desire to communicate whenever they take part in Mass, the sacrament of penance has recovered its own particular value. If in the early Church it was essentially the rite of reconciliation of those who had been excommunicated and, as such, the condition in effect for their admission to communion, the practice of frequent confession, of confessions of devotion, which began to be introduced into the Church at an early date under the influence of monasticism, ought logically to contribute to a consideration of this sacrament in itself and independently of the Eucharist.

In fact, it is exactly the opposite which has occurred. The distinction between confession of devotion and the sacrament of reconciliation of the excommunicated has become blurred in the minds of the faithful who in the end have come to regard themselves in practice as "excommunicated". Hence those Masses celebrated at which no one dares to communicate because they have not been to confession immediately beforehand.

Hence also in the minds of very many Christians, the idea of fulfilling the Easter precept is primarily one of going to confession.

This confession, moreover, is less and less regarded as a sacrament. The "confessional" is the last stage of an evolution which has succeeded in conferring on it a private character. The liturgy of the sacrament for this very reason has become increasingly rudimentary. A biologist would be tempted to say that nowadays it was scarcely more than a "vestigial organ". In the view of the ordinary Christian it is a question, fundamentally, of giving an exact account of all his sins to the priest. The insistence laid, even lately, on the integrity of the confession, is of particular significance in this respect. Hence, also, the importance attached increasingly to the freedom of choice of confessor by the penitent, a slender palliative to the repugnance that he can feel at undergoing this disagreeable formality. But all this contributes to making confession much more an interview with a priest, which can turn into direction of conscience, than a sacrament, that is, an encounter with God in the joy of redemption.

The last remaining memory of Christian feeling subsisting among dechristianized masses is the idea that a sacrament is a celebration. There is a celebration on the occasion of a marriage, a baptism. The one sacrament that seems to have lost this particular note is the sacrament of penance. Yet "there is more rejoicing in heaven over one sinner who repents. . . ." The sacrament of penance, like the other sacraments, is a sacrament of redemption, an invention of the redemptive love of Christ. It seems that to bring back the general run of Christians to greater awareness of the reality of faith, the sacrament of penance must be restored, in one form or another, to its ecclesial and community dimensions. If, in considering our sins, we feel the need to invoke the intervention of the authorities of the Church, it is because we have become aware of everything that can have impaired our relationship with the Church at the same time as with God; in these conditions, the priest would not be regarded so much as the one who is charged with the resolution of cases of conscience but as the minister of a sacrament.

But to do that it would also be necessary to restore the whole penitential liturgy. Certain essays of this sort have been made. It may well be thought that the state of mind from which the liturgical renewal of our times derives, as it becomes increasingly more marked, will furnish a major contribution towards the creation of a climate of opinion that will bring about the disappearance of certain misconceptions and ensure a better understanding of the function of penance in Christian life. And it is possible that the reformed rite of penance, called for by the Second Vatican Council will reflect some of the *desiderata* mentioned above.

MARRIAGE

The same liturgical problem is raised by marriage and the need for liturgical renewal is felt also in this field.

That this is so illustrates obviously one of the characteristics of our times. In a civilization in which the frequency of divorce cases causes one to think of a real collapse of the family as an institution, where social customs evolve under the pressure of a world where the distribution of work between the sexes is very different from what it formerly was, it is hardly surprising that a vigorous and healthy reaction should provoke the formation of family movements, of communities of families and of a thorough re-examination of the whole concept of family spirituality. In this context, which is peculiar to our own period, must be situated the investigation into the pastoral problems of marriage.

Traditionally, the rites of marriage were so to say embedded in a whole context of customs and usages varying from one region to another wherein were mingled together the sacred and the profane. But all this social structure has today suddenly broken down. A great gap has appeared which requires to be filled at the very time when the problem of the family appears with a clarity and a gravity that are entirely new. Here, once more, the spirit of the liturgical renewal must normally find expression in parallel investigations and endeavours in the different countries. The United States, Belgium, Germany and Ireland have obtained approval for a new rite of marriage. Here again, it is when marriage is no longer considered solely as a contract between two individuals that the rite takes on its full meaning: it is a moment in the life of the whole parochial community and the nuptial Mass is therefore no longer a "private" Mass, but the community as a whole shares in it. A time will come no doubt when, as in the young communities of missionary countries, the succession of marriages, one after another in the same church throughout a whole morning, each with its "own" Mass, attended only by those who have come out of social habit or regard for the families who have "ordered" it, will be unknown.

CONCLUSION

If we attempt to state clearly the general characteristics of this liturgical renewal, as they are shown on the different occasions that we have just considered, one thing seems to emerge very clearly: this is the striking importance attached to the rôle of the community as a whole. In certain country parishes where there is only one Mass on Sundays the custom has been introduced of administering baptism in the presence of the congregation gathered for this Mass. The community character of the sacrament is brought out particularly at the Easter vigil and the catechumenate for adults will certainly take this into account: preparation for baptism in fact to be efficacious presupposes that the catechumen is in touch not only with the priest and godparents but also with the Christian community which is to receive him in its midst. The rite of the baptism of adults, indeed, makes provision for these three contingencies. The extent to which its real significance is realized will lead to proportionate emphasis being given to the different stages of the catechumenate, by the scrutinies required by the Ritual which will be carried out in the presence of the assembled community where the priest and godparents have both their own rôles to play.

This question of godparents and of entry into the community recurs in connection with confirmation. Here again the spirit of authenticity which is a characteristic of the liturgical renewal is in opposition to the unmeaning formality which consists in designating more or less arbitrarily a collective "godparent" for a whole number of candidates. If on principle the godparent at confirmation should be different from that of baptism, in accordance with a custom still mentioned expressly in canon law (can. 796, §1), there is some advantage in letting the child, who could not be consulted at the time of his baptism, freely ratify at this stage the choice then made in his name or, on the other hand, without of course ignoring the advice of his natural educators, in allowing him to choose another godparent in a position to help him more effectively. Ordinarily this problem should arouse the conscience of the Christian community as a whole in the case of children who cannot find in their own families that climate of faith which they need; in these very frequent cases it is through the child and on the occasion of his confirmation that the whole family should be taken into sponsorship by a member of the community who fully realizes his missionary rôle as a witness to the faith.

A similar problem occurs in connection with marriage. Allusion has already been made to the pre-marriage courses in which certain married couples are called on to give the benefit of their experience to the engaged couples. In certain cases, could not the official witness to a marriage act as a sort of godparent whose rôle might find expression in the rite of marriage? Those educators who are closely in touch with the psychological difficulties of the victims of marital or family instability in the modern world, are fully aware how important it is to show them, in their immediate surroundings, really successful marriages. Frequentation of a genuinely happy home can very often exert a decisive influence on the development of young couples in difficulties of one sort or another. We have here, indeed, an example of how older couples can assume some responsibility for younger ones—a state of affairs which should be regarded as quite normal and which, when it is done with the necessary tact and respect, should find its clear expression in the liturgical and pastoral renewal of the Church in our days. Here again, sponsorship by individuals is in direct relationship with the concern of the whole community for the special needs of each of its members.

CHAPTER X

THE FUTURE OF THE LITURGICAL MOVEMENT

If it is forbidden to envisage a religious syncretism at the doctrinal level, is it allowed to envisage a liturgical syncretism? At a period of extreme political and administrative centralization like our own, in which the phenomenon of acculturation is no less manifest, is a universal liturgy out of the question— a liturgy which would be the reduction to a common denominator and to the best of their elements of the principal Christian liturgies in existence? Can we dream of such a universal liturgy which would be adapted and presented to each human group in accordance with its cultural differences, in its own language, with those elements common to all in one language, Latin the language of the Roman Church, Greek or Hebrew as languages of the Revelation, Aramaic as our Lord's own language?

Such a dream, which some will not fail to find utopian, could not in any case be realized by a team of scholars, specialists in the ancient and modern history of the liturgy, nor by a central administrative body, even if it were composed of the various qualified representatives of all the Churches of the East and West. These artificial methods of work have never, in the whole history of Christian worship, furnished anything but mediocre and somewhat negative results, to the detriment of a natural development as diversified as the beliefs which have been its cause.

And so we believe that in this natural movement of religious evolution, and so far as we can dare to foretell the future, the liturgical movement will go forward in a twofold direction, at once divergent and complementary, despite the inherent contradiction in this statement.

It will go forward in the direction of a certain freedom which, there is no denying it and whatever certain grumbling critics may think, is one of the fundamental advances of our times. And so the liturgical movement must lead to the evolution of greatly diversified forms following the various countries and human groups, since to express its faith and worship religious inspiration must draw even on popular folklore and, of course, on the different cultures.

On the other hand, in the context of an ever more rapid internationalization, this faith and worship, while respecting legitimate local forms of expression, must come to common expressions which will not be a synthesis of local forms. Culture has never been a collection of local folklores cunningly put together by certain talented persons for whom the whole is formed by a simple addition of the parts. In the same way, a universal expression of divine worship can very well be based on a vital sense of tradition—and this has nothing to do with an archeological inventory of the same tradition. No more than religious thought can develop on the basis of Denzinger's *Enchiridion*, the universal liturgy of the future Church will not be built up on the basis of a synthesis of the liturgical renewal even extended to the whole Church.

In the establishment of this liturgy the principal rôle will obviously fall to the Roman Church, considered not only as the mistress of all other Churches, but as developing within herself as a local Church (the diocese of Rome) forms of worship suitable as formerly (for example, the Roman liturgy of the fourth century) to be adopted into the framework of a genuinely Catholic liturgy. But history has witnessed more than one example of a local liturgy, one, so to say, without authority at the beginning, spreading to the whole of the Church, or to a large part of the Church. Not to mention the apostolic Churches of the East, even in the West there are examples of liturgies which have not only preserved their local customs but have passed them on to other communities.

It seems likely that the future will respect and develop this beneficial ecclesial tradition. In a legitimate diversification of liturgies (it is obvious that at the present time the dispute over the Chinese rites would be unthinkable) the liturgy of the Church will be the realization, under the authority of Rome, of a harmonized synthesis of what "the Spirit will say to the Churches".

Outstanding in the liturgical Constitution of the Second Vatican Council are the provisions for the adaptation of the liturgy to different peoples and cultures. The relevant paragraphs, some of which have already been mentioned, dealing with the use of the vernacular and the reform of the liturgical books, carry the proposed adaptation to a certain stage, but it is paragraph 40 under the general heading of "Principles for the adaptation of the liturgy to the culture and tradition of nations" which is particularly to the point in this connection: "In certain places and circumstances, however, an even more radical adaptation of the liturgy is needed." It does not disguise the difficulties facing such an endeavour and, consequently, lays down careful rules to be followed and allows experiments to be undertaken for a limited period of time among groups specially suited for the purpose.

EASTERN RITES

In the ecumenical sphere and following the general lines of the movement, the attention given to non-Latin Christian Churches is an important factor of the liturgical renewal. This has already been mentioned in Part II of this book. To the extent that ecumenism consists, for all Churches, in the rediscovery of a certain Christian authenticity, the liturgy, which is a privileged means for this return to authenticity, must itself be inspired by it.

Here we may mention more particularly the family of Eastern Churches in the Near and Middle East in communion

with Rome. These Churches, which have their own liturgical
and national languages and employ living languages in their
eucharistic celebrations, use French as their principal cultural
language. Since all the seminaries in the Middle East for the
past two generations or more have been under the direction
of French religious, the principal review concerning these communities (*Proche-Orient Chrétien*) is published by the White
Fathers of St Anne's seminary in Jerusalem, that concerning
more especially the Churches of Syrian (liturgical) language
(*L'Orient Syrien*) is published in Paris and, a fact of particular
significance, the first Byzantine "Missal" for the use of the
faithful, which was recently published at Alexandria, was in
French; an Arabic translation appeared afterwards.

None of the foregoing affects the fact that these various
communities really belong, at the cultural and ethnical levels,
to the world in which they live, in which they seek not only
not to be submerged but to contribute to its opening to the rest
of mankind. On the other hand, sufficient advantage has not
been taken of the phenomenon of acculturation, which is being emphasized here. This applies to both sides, to the East
and the West; it could lead to a better communion between the
Churches and more fruitful mutual aid in what concerns us
here, that is, the liturgical field. If we are no longer in that
period when Eastern liturgies, celebrated on the occasion of the
weeks of prayer for Christian unity, provided an attractive
and perhaps somewhat exotic spectacle for some of the faithful of the Roman rite, it does not appear that serious consideration has been given to the liturgical traditions of the
East, despite the efforts of the White Fathers at St Anne's or
the Benedictines of Amay-Chevetogne. These traditions, in
fact, have made little progress among the liturgists of the
present period. What the Eastern Churches desire is no longer
to be regarded as if they were, so to say, dependents on the
"Colonial Office" but to be treated as if they were fully allied
States. It is certainly to be hoped that the tradition on this
point represented by Dom Guéranger (see chapter I, footnote
2, p. 12) will no longer prevail anywhere and that comparative

liturgy, as revived scientifically by Baumstark, will gain a large following.

Fr Bouyer deplores the practical non-existence of canonical study of the liturgy. He does so very rightly on the basis of the theological content, the spiritual structure and the pastoral setting of the liturgy. There are, he says, a number of rubrical commentaries on the liturgy, but these, however useful they may be,

> bear about the same relation to a canonical study of the liturgy that cook-books bear to a treatise on the chemistry of food. Indeed, cook-books have a great advantage over handbooks of ceremonies—when you have some practical experience in cooking and follow their advice quite blindly, you can produce very good dishes even though you do not know why; but blindly following handbooks of ceremonies—because of their purely logical and superficial way of solving questions—will give you only a worship which is apparently correct but may be intrinsically dead.[1]

Here may be added a complementary desideratum in connection with the elaboration of this canonical study of the liturgy that is necessary. For the universal Church it could only be the fruit, at the starting-point, of a systematic comparison extended to all the traditions of worship in existence in the Church and of methodical examination of the concept of the sacred and the constants of the religious mind, both individual and communal.

Secondly, without taking into account questions of law, missionaries have reached the conclusion that knowledge of rites different from those of the Latin Church could be of great use for those among them who intend to establish the Church in places that have not yet, or only partially, been evangelized. They have even come to advocate the adoption of this or that oriental rite in a region where it has already been in use for a long time (as in India) or its extension to another region which by political circumstances is placed in, or has returned to,

[1] Bouyer, *op. cit.*, p. 280.

a cultural sphere also endowed with one or several rites (the case of North Africa in relationship with the Arab world as a whole is relevant here). The variation in political conditions, on the one hand, and the variety of rites, which entails disadvantages, on the other, calls for very great circumspection in this field.

Nevertheless, there can only be praise and gratitude for all those, priests, isolated religious or entire religious communities, who, according to local circumstances, have adopted a rite different from their own. This attitude is an undeniable manifestation of a genuinely spiritual and ecclesial point of view. The Christian East has nothing analogous, or so little to propose, in answer to the Western Church that can prove so living and valuable, except for the fact that the Eastern tradition accommodates itself more easily than does the Latin tradition to the countries to which it spreads, and thus, after all, can offer comparison with the principle which appears to inspire the passage of a Latin to an Eastern rite—that is, to pray in the language and rites of the communities among whom we are or, in the absence of these rites, with those of the communities nearest to them.

In any case, great caution is needed here; the natural play of sympathies and affinities, must be given free rein and a watchful eye must be kept on the evolution of peoples and societies as we look towards a future which depends on the Church, to the extent that we believe that she alone is capable of building up on the ruins of present nationalisms and imperialisms a new civilization for a humanity reconciled together at last.

THE PROBLEM OF AFRICANIZATION

The problem of adaptation occurs particularly, as we have seen, in missionary countries, and it is in these that the radical adaptation foreseen by the liturgical Constitution will probably take place. In this connection, a report drawn up by Dom Thierry Maertens, a few years before the Council met, is relevant here. He was describing a journey of liturgical research undertaken in Africa. He writes:

The problem of Africanization of the liturgy is certainly one of those which gives most concern to the Church in Africa, particularly to the African priests. It is a delicate problem and presupposes that those who study it have an accurate idea of what is God's part and what is man's in the liturgy. Everywhere I held study sessions or lectures I was concerned, in order to determine the limits of Africanization, to distinguish between the *biblical* rites, giving expression to God's primordial and untouchable plan, and the *cultural* or *catechetical* elements which constitute the setting for the former. The liturgy is primarily a supernatural work whose expression must be sought in the will of God as it is principally to be found in Scripture. This supernatural work encounters and transforms a human psychology; it is therefore only normal that this supernatural psychology should also find its expression in the liturgy. From this twofold form of expression—supernatural and human— in the liturgy springs a pastoral method which is in a state of continual tension between two poles and the balance is not always easy to achieve. Before the more recent Roman directives Europe experienced certain tendencies which emphasized the supernatural, even to the point of neglecting the pastoral side, and also tendencies urging a form of adaptation in which man and his complexes became the final criterion of liturgical symbolism. The same tension occurs in Africa and I have often been tempted to label some experiment that I have encountered as being excessively human or excessively supernatural. On occasion Africanization runs the risk of falling into the former category. It is important then for agreement to be reached on the limits of Africanization.

In the first place, a clear distinction must be made between work of liturgical Africanization and the present national movements. Both are good and praiseworthy and it is quite right that Christians and their priests should be simultaneously concerned about both problems. But it is not suitable that the liturgical problem should be presented in the nationalist context. Africanization is a cause with arguments at its disposal which are far more theological and ecclesial. In all truth I feel bound to say how greatly I was impressed by the excellent judgment of the African clergy in this matter.

Then, Africanization is not, and cannot be merely a question of ritual. It is no part of the Church's mission to save customary rites from disappearance, as if her liturgy were a museum full of fine pieces. An African rite can have a chance of incorporation only to the extent that it remains expressive of a living community that can be supernaturalized. Now in many regions several rites have been carefully recorded by ethnologists that are gradually disappearing under the influence of Europeanization and modernization, especially in the cities which will control the form taken by the future face of Africa.

At the present time there is a considerable urge towards "negritude". It should be encouraged and fostered. But it will encounter such difficulties in the Europeanized centres that the Church can only commit herself to this trend with infinite prudence. She will probably limit, for the time being at any rate, the possibilities of Africanization to paraliturgical ceremonies.

Lastly, Africanization will demand the undertaking of numerous works of research and important pastoral experiments. A too enthusiastic approach might lead to it being thought that the whole of the liturgical renewal in Africa consisted in this work. It would be a grievous error excessively to "humanize" the work of Christ. It is desirable, therefore, that those who are concerned with the Africanization of rites should also be those who develop the biblical catechesis of these same rites, thus "initiating" the African to liturgical life at the same time as they "adapt" certain elements of the liturgy to the African religious mind. Priests trained in this twofold task will be really able to do useful work in pastoral liturgy. . . .

The whole of this report is worthy of quotation and particularly the part which follows on the possibilities in the way of Africanization together with what is said, in speaking of general principles, of everything concerning the community work of liturgy in Negro Africa, the importance of the proclamation of the Word of God within the act of worship and finally the special possibilities that seem to be offered to the

African Church in the matter of singing, following the special gifts of their peoples.

SOUTH AMERICA

It is also important to point out what is being done in one part of the Church where the ecumenical problem crops up in terms different from Europe and where missionary needs are felt as acutely, and sometimes more acutely, than in missionary countries in the proper sense of the term. The importance of Latin America, in the eyes of the universal Church and in a general view of the present evolution of the world, hardly requires emphasis.

In a paper read at the Nijmegen missionary conference in 1955, Mgr Larrain, bishop of Talca in Chile, speaking on the urgency for liturgical renewal in Latin America, examined the situation there in some detail. His conclusion was that for the faith to be revitalized there the missionary must be prepared to face widespread religious ignorance, lack of understanding of the Church and an alarming shortage of priests. The source of these troubles, he considered, might well lie in not having given sufficient emphasis to liturgical life among Latin Americans.

> It was Geoffrey Kurth who said fifty years ago that the liturgy lived is a solution to the social problems of men. In it we find the organic and vital sense of the collective. In it we come to understand the meaning of *social* when we say "we" and not "me". In it and by it we enter into communion with our brothers in Jesus Christ. In it we overcome the individualistic view of human affairs in favour of the value of the social outlook. But if such values are to be inculcated in Latin America then we must have a liturgical renewal. The liturgy, without losing any of its traditional richness where our own lives and the history of the Church express themselves, must be adapted to our contemporary lives.[2]

Mgr Larrain called for a threefold adaptation, and in doing

[2] Johannes Hofinger, S.J. (Editor), *Liturgy and the Missions* (London and New York, 1960), pp. 93–5.

so anticipated the liturgical Constitution. In the first place the liturgy must be adapted to the present historical situation. If the Christian tradition of the Middle Ages, especially in what concerns active participation in liturgical life, poses a problem for Latin America whose culture stems from Western civilization, how much greater is the problem in Asia and Africa where no such Western tradition has influenced the native cultures. How impersonal and remote must liturgy be that is unadapted to such peoples. Secondly, there must be psychological adaptation, adaptation, that is, to the mentality of the people. And lastly there must be adaptation of language. Mgr Larrain called for a far greater use of the vernacular. Despite its name, in Latin America there is unfortunately no Latin tradition.... Latin is taught only in the seminaries. Even the cultured classes, to say nothing of the average people, know nothing of Latin as a language. Such adaptation, Mgr Larrain concluded, "will contribute much to the missionary's work of evangelization, and restore to the Catholic faith in Latin America the vitality and dynamism it needs".

THE LITURGICAL CONSTITUTION OF THE SECOND VATICAN COUNCIL

It is fitting that this book, which gives an account of the history, development and basic requirements of the liturgical movement, should conclude with a chapter on the liturgical Constitution passed by the Second Vatican Council (the Constitution was promulgated on December 4th, 1963), for even a superficial examination of it shows that most of the requirements of the liturgical movement as outlined in the previous chapters have been met. Indeed, it is some indication of the penetration among bishops of the Church of the fundamental ideas governing the movement that the Constitution was voted at the Council by so overwhelming a majority (2,147 in favour, four against). As has already been made clear in this book, the last fifty years, with the rapid evolution of modern society, have shown the increasing and acute need for liturgical reform; that this should be the first reform to be voted by the Council was a sign not only of its urgency but also of the importance of the liturgy in the life of the Church. It is, as the Constitution makes clear, "both the summit to which her action tends and the fount whence springs all her strength"; the liturgy is spoken of (in the words of the Secret of the ninth Sunday after Pentecost) as that "through which the work of our redemption is wrought" (*opus nostrae redemptionis exercetur*). As such, therefore, it concerns every member of the Church, for the liturgy, as the Constitution points out, is the "place" of man's social encounter with Christ, just as private prayer is the occasion of an individual encounter. And the two are not exclusive, for public worship should lead to private prayer just as private prayer leads to public worship.

A little more than four hundred years ago the Council of Trent, before concluding its long series of sessions, came to consider the question of worship; various projects for reform were put forward, but time was pressing and finally the whole matter was left to be dealt with by the pope. As a consequence, during the next half century or so a reformed edition of each of the liturgical books was issued, the last being the Roman Ritual in 1614, which was, in fact, a new creation. In this way the chaotic state of the Church's public worship at the end of the medieval period was remedied, but the reformed liturgy that emerged, inevitably perhaps in view of prevailing circumstances, seemed to be conceived as an entirely clerical affair. The Congregation of Rites, established in 1587, in addition to emphasizing this clerical aspect, contrived to create the impression that liturgy was an affair of rubrical interpretation solely and that it was changeless and unchangeable. And so the ritualism which had developed during the medieval period, while shorn of some of its more exuberant features, was by no means entirely banished; indeed for the next three and a half centuries it tended to increase. Some rites, which in the sixteenth century had already begun to lose much of their significance for the people in church, by the end of the nineteenth were almost completely devoid of meaning for the majority of the clergy and laity. It is true that, as we have seen, a certain amount of tinkering was done during the first half of this century but it was clear that these measures were only of a temporary character intended to lead to a thoroughgoing reform.

In general, like the Council of Trent, the Second Vatican

Council has been content to state the general principles on which the reform should proceed and to leave their practical application to the competent commission entrusted with the reform of the liturgical books. Nevertheless, in parts of the Constitution the Council has been careful to indicate some of the detailed applications of its decrees.

Yet more striking than the actual measures for reform are general statements of principles concerning the nature of the liturgy and the people's part in it. More clearly and authoritatively than ever before it is laid down that if the Church's worship is to have its full effect the congregation is to take an informed, active and fruitful part (*scienter, actuose et fructuose*), and it is for this reason that the liturgical books are to be reformed, so that the rites may more clearly express their meaning. The rites are to be of noble simplicity, avoiding useless repetitions, and not needing much explanation; to the same end, a more varied and more suitable selection of Scripture passages is to be chosen.

Obviously the various rites will express their meaning more clearly if they are in the language of the congregation, and so a wide concession has been made for the translation of the liturgy into modern languages. Its application has been left, very properly, to the judgement of local hierarchies, but it is the admission of the principle that is important, that there is no intrinsic reason why the Church's worship should be conducted in a dead language, or why the sacramental forms should not be heard and understood by those for whom they are intended.

For Mass, in addition to the permission for the vernacular for the common part (roughly, whatever is said aloud or sung), the principal change is the introduction of the "prayer of the faithful"—or rather its restoration after something like fourteen hundred years. This general prayer is still in use, of course, on Good Friday under the form of the solemn collects. Its place is immediately after the Gospel and sermon. The rite of Mass is to be reformed with a view to greater simplicity and to enable the congregation to take a fuller part. The duplications which have crept in in the course of centuries are to be eliminated. We are not told what these are but the repetitious prayers at the Offertory, the saying by the celebrant of what is sung by the congregation, the conflict between the prayers at the foot of the altar and the entrance chant are all matters that seem to call for simplification. Once again, a strong recommendation is made that the congregation should receive communion from hosts consecrated at the Mass at which they are present. Pius XII mentioned this twice in the Encyclical *Mediator* (1947) without, it must be confessed, very much success.

The permission for concelebration on certain occasions will at least ensure that the difficulties attending celebration of Mass at places like Lourdes, or during congresses with many priests present, will be greatly diminished, with a consequent increase of reverence; where the practice is introduced, with the bishop's permission, in monasteries and cathedral chapters, it will give new significance to the conventual or chapter Mass which, nowadays, seems to have lost much of its meaning when those for whom it is intended have already communicated or celebrated at an earlier hour.

In the chapter on the sacraments emphasis is again given to the need for the people to understand (*maxime ... interest ut fideles signa sacramentorum intellegant*: "it is of extreme importance that the faithful should understand the sacramental signs"). The restoration of the catechumenate with its stages clearly marked by the successive rites pertaining to it (at present grouped together in the rite of baptism), the stress laid on confirmation as part of Christian initiation, the statement that the anointing of the sick is to be so called and that it comes before Viaticum, the promised reform of the rites of penance and of funerals, are all signs that the Council has appreciated to the full the pastoral inadequacies of the *Rituale Romanum*.

On the Breviary the Council has been more explicit about the features of the reform. After emphasizing that the Hours are meant to correspond with the times of day at which they are celebrated, the Constitution lays down that Lauds and

Vespers are the principal Hours of the Office (a return to the primitive conception of the old Roman Office before the monastic influence predominated) and are so to be celebrated. Prime is abolished (and with it, presumably, the Martyrology as a liturgical book). Terce, Sext and None remain, but in private recitation one of them may be chosen, in accordance with the time of day, and the two others omitted. Matins retains its place in choir as *nocturna laus,* but it is to be so re-arranged that it can be recited privately at any convenient time of day and is to contain longer lessons and fewer psalms. Weekly recitation of the psalter is abolished and the psalms are to be distributed over a longer period. What this period will be remains a question. The present Ambrosian Breviary has a fortnightly scheme, the Breviary of the Humiliati in the sixteenth century had a monthly one.

It does not appear that the form of the Office will be changed in order to differentiate between public and private recitation, as some authorities have asked. After all, the Church's Office is one and whether said alone or sung solemnly in choir it remains the public praise and prayer of the community, the Mystical Body, whose members, our Lord said, he came to lead as "true adorers to the Father".

There is an important chapter of the Constitution on the liturgical year, emphasizing once again the pre-eminence of the proper of the season over the sanctoral. The latter is to be still further reduced so that only those saints appear in the general calendar of the Roman rite who are of universal importance; those of local interest are to be commemorated only in the places where there is special reason for their veneration— where they worked, their native place, and so on. In this way the celebration of the seasonal liturgy will be emphasized with the Sunday and ferial Office predominating over that of the saints. The ferial Office will become, in fact, the usual one and that of the saints the exception. This is a principle that liturgical reformers have been endeavouring to apply for some centuries, Pius V and Benedict XIV among them.

Although it has been impossible to do more than mention

very summarily the chief points of so long and important a document it will have emerged clearly enough that the first definitive result of the Council constitutes a major liturgical reform, more radical and far-reaching than that of Trent. It is not yet complete, of course, and to appreciate its full implications we shall have to wait for the reformed liturgical books. How long will that be? It took the liturgical commission, set up by the pope after Trent, five years for the production of a Breviary and seven for a Missal. Nowadays, no doubt, with greater knowledge and, probably, a more advanced stage of preparation, the waiting period should be shorter. Some of the reforms have been introduced already before the publication of the new books. In France, Belgium, Germany, Canada and the United States, arrangements were made for a certain amount of the vernacular to be used at Mass (for example, for the lessons) and came into force practically at the same time as the Constitution (February 16th, 1964).

The far-reaching extent of the reform requires much more than just the translation of some rites or the preparation of new editions of Missal, Breviary, Ritual and Pontifical. It calls indeed for a fundamental change of attitude on the part of many clergy and laity towards the whole idea of liturgy. That which has generally or at least popularly prevailed hitherto, is, it can now be seen, inadequate; in its place is required something with a different emphasis and outlook. Those who have worked, not without opposition, for a restoration of the Church's worship to its proper place and function and have tried to promote a better understanding of it will be greatly encouraged by this Constitution, for it seems that what has come to be known as the liturgical movement has achieved at one stroke all that it has been working for for some fifty years. But it is of great importance that December 4th, 1963, should not now be regarded by this movement as the height of its achievement but rather as the first rung on the ladder towards it. For the reform to be effective an immense work of education of clergy and laity will have to be carried out under the leadership of the bishops; indeed without it, especially in those countries where far too little of the necessary preliminary theological spadework has yet been done, there is small chance of the reform achieving its end.

It has been pointed out that this is a disciplinary and not a dogmatic decree of the Council. But the theological implications of the Constitution, particularly of its introductory section on the nature of liturgy, are many. Essentially there is nothing new, the fundamentals of Catholic worship remain what they were before—that is obvious—but it will be a new image that is presented to the world, new because the old post-medieval, post-Tridentine image no longer spoke to the modern world, and after all it is the modern world which has to receive the Christian message through the Church's worship.

SELECT BIBLIOGRAPHY

In this series: AMIOT, François: *History of the Mass*; DENIS-BOULET, Nöele M.: *The Christian Calendar*; DALMAIS, Irenée-Henri, O.P.: *The Eastern Liturgies*; SHEPPARD, Lancelot C.: *The Liturgical Books.*

BARRY, Colman J.: *Worship and Work*, Collegeville, Minn., Liturgical Press, 1956.

BAUMSTARK, Anton: *Comparative Liturgy*, London, Mowbray, and Westminster, Md, Newman Press, 1958.

BOUYER, Louis: *The Paschal Mystery*, London, Allen & Unwin, 1951; *Liturgical Piety* (U.S. edn; English edn, *Liturgy and Life*), Notre Dame, Ind., Univ. of Notre Dame Press, 1955, and London, Sheed & Ward, 1958.

CASEL, Odo, O.S.B.: *The Mystery of Christian Worship*, London, Darton, Longman & Todd, and Westminster, Md, Newman Press, 1962.

DAVIS, Charles: *Liturgy and Doctrine*, London and New York, Sheed & Ward, 1960.

EISENHOFER, Ludwig, and LECHNER, Joseph: *The Liturgy of the Roman Rite*, Edinburgh, Nelson, and New York, Herder & Herder, 1961.

HOFINGER, Johannes, S.J. (Editor): *Liturgy and the Missions: The Nijmegen Papers*, London, Burns & Oates, and New York, Kenedy, 1960.

JUNGMANN, Joseph Andreas, S.J.: *The Mass of the Roman Rite, Its Origins and Development* (Missarum Solemnia), translated by F. A. Brunner, C.SS.R. Two volumes. New York, Benziger, 1951 and 1955.

KLAUSER, Theodor: *The Western Liturgy*, London, Mowbray, 1952.

KOENKER, E. B.: *The Liturgical Renaissance in the Roman Catholic Church*, Chicago, Univ. of Chicago Press, 1954.

KOROLEVSKY, C.: *Living Languages in Catholic Worship*, translated by Donald Attwater, London and New York, Longmans, 1957.

MARCO, Angelus A. de, O.F.M.: *Rome and the Vernacular*, Westminster, Md, Newman Press, 1961.

MURPHY, John L.: *The Mass and Liturgical Reform*, Milwaukee, Bruce, 1957.

MURRAY, Placid, O.S.B. (Editor): *Studies in Pastoral Liturgy*, Maynooth, The Furrow Trust, 1961.

NOCENT, Adrien: *The Future of the Liturgy*, New York, Herder & Herder, 1963.

O'CONNELL, J. B.: *Sacred Music and Liturgy* (the Instruction of the S. Congregation of Rites, translated with a commentary), London, Burns & Oates, 1959.

ROUSSEAU, Dom Olivier, O.S.B.: *Progress of the Liturgy*, Westminster, Md, Newman Press, 1951.

RYAN, Vincent, O.S.B. (Editor): *Studies in Pastoral Liturgy*, Maynooth, The Furrow Trust, 1963.

The Twentieth Century
Encyclopedia of Catholicism

The number of each volume indicates its place in the over-all series and not the order of publication.

PART ONE: KNOWLEDGE AND FAITH

PART TWO: THE BASIC TRUTHS

All titles are subject to change.